Satan is in Sales

Satan Is In sales

Understanding the Strategy of the Enemy.

Michael Canion

Revised January 10, 2018

By Michael Canion

For information contact :

http://www.bmcanion.org

404-228-6969

Book cover by Exodus Design.

ISBN-9781986867153

First Edition : August 1996

WHAT PEOPLE ARE SAYING.

After reading "Satan is in Sales", I took full inventory of my own life. I wanted to be sure that I was not purchasing anything the salesman was peddling. This book made me think, really think, and it will do the same for you. Reading "Satan is in Sales" was a reminder of how smooth, cunning, and subtle, Satan was and still is.

 This book is a must read for all pastors and their congregants, because among our congregants, Satan is peddling his wares daily. This book will really help pastors better equip the people against the strategies of the salesman.

 And to Bishop Michael Canion, I want to say I thank God for speaking to you and giving you the vision, information and inspiration to write such a book as this. You have always been a visionary for the Body of Christ and writing this book is just another way that God is using you to be a blessing to the body. I pray that God will continue to use you to be a worldwide inspiration.

Bishop Anthony Dixon
Word Alive Ministry

"Those in ministry have a number of responsibilities. When Paul address this subject is Ephesians 4:12, he includes "perfecting or equipping the saints." Bishop Canion has done a masterful job of equipping the saints to be spiritually victorious. We are in spiritual warfare and need spiritual strategies for spiritual victory. In this book, Bishop Canion provides these strategies. Clearly, we need these strategies.

In John 10:10, Jesus warns of the enemy's purposes to kill, steal, and destroy. In 2 Corinthians 2:11, the Apostle Paul teaches us not to be ignorant, when it comes to the enemy's devices. Finally, Paul also tells us, in Ephesians 2:27, not to give place to the enemy.

In this book, Bishop Canion exposes the adversary's methodologies. He skillfully arms the believers on how not to give the devil space or opportunity to act in our lives. Bishop Canion has proficiently used a profession we all are familiar with to expose the ways of the enemy. This is a must read for every child of God who desires spiritual victory."

Pastor Arthur Mosley
Cathedral of Faith C.O.G.I.C.

The vision, purpose, and plan of a sales person is to encourage someone to buy something whether they need it or not. As you read this book you will come to realize that Satan is the ultimate salesman, and at one time or another we have all made purchases.

What a wonderful time for a book such as this one to be published. Satan is in Sales warns us but it goes further and equips us, so that we are not ignorant of the strategies of Satan.

Bishop Canion, in writing this book is our present-day Paul Revere warning us that our enemy is coming. Our present-day John the Baptist saying repent for the Kingdom of God is at hand. Our present-day Prophet exposing the works and plans of the devil. This book is a must read.

Bishop Artis Crum
Light and Salvation Outreach Church

As a former salesman myself, it was difficult to distinguish the difference between deceptive manipulation and honest conviction. This book exposes the ploy of the enemy, as convincing as he may appear at times, of the true nature of his sales pitch. Confidence men must first win your trust before they are able to sell you their goods. Bishop Michael Canion presents a clear picture of how easy it is for Satan's victims to fall captive to his traps. The personal stories shared with us through Bishop Canion's transparency drive home the realness of this ongoing battle for the souls of men. I advise all who read this book to also take inventory of their own lives so that they can become more fully aware of the doors yet open to the enemy's devises so that God's Word may become the absolute Source from which all choices are made.

Woodrow Walker
Senior Pastor of Cross Culture Church

This is a strong analogy describing Satan as a sales expert. The explanations are straightforward. The examples are practical and produce impactful imagery. It is scripturally and theologically sound. I thought the section of "fetal sin" was insightful.

The suggestion to proceed with action because sin has already occurred in the heart is a frequent (lethal) approach by the salesman, however, this distinction is seldom captured well in teaching and preaching.

The sales presentation inspires consideration, contemplation and meditation. I recommend this book to anyone.

Richard Woods
Chief Advisory Officer
Sacred Fire Ministries

FORWARD FOR SATAN IS IN SALES

Although I am married to this brilliant man, he never ceases to amaze me. He has the ability to take complicated matters and simplify them into every day, practical terms, so that everyone understands them.

Many people have fallen prey to the temptations that Satan dangles on a daily basis. He uses the thirst for power, prestige and pride as a springboard to launch an assault on the mind.

This book is written to sound the alarm and call for a mass awakening of Satan's tactics. Satan's goals are not to just harm you, but to actually destroy you and all that is connected to you. John 10:10 warns us that the enemy comes to steal, kill and to destroy. Satanic tactics are shrewd and cunning. We often miss them because they are so subtle. Most of the time, he does not come at once but his approaches are small and consistent. He does it that way so that you are not aware, he has mastered deception.

Bishop Michael Canion paints a picture and wonderfully illustrates in this book how crafty Satan really is. In this book, he gives insight into overcoming the grip Satan has on many lives, and he helps the reader overcome and understand temptation. Consistently woven in these narratives is the urgency to use discernment and to walk daily in the Spirit of God.

Bishop Canion further provokes us to intensify our grip on God and to never let go of His hand, in order that we may avoid the trapping of Satan. He provides the reader with tools for living everyday victorious lives through Christ which gives us strength.

Bishop Michael Canion gives a step by step strategic plan to conquer the enemy of our souls. Satan is in Sales is a must read. This book is a one of a kind inspiration and instructional aide for those who want to walk in victory on a daily basis.

A Woman for Whom Christ Died,

Dr. Tanda Joy Canion, Co-Pastor
Assembly of Truth Family Worship Center
Founder of:
Tanda Canion Ministries
Tanda Canion Foundation
Panache National Women's Group

Acknowledgement

I would like to thank my wife who is one of the most gifted individuals I know. She is a great wife, mother, grandmother and coworker in the ministry. She has added to my life beyond my ability to articulate. You are a phenomenal woman who is known for your excellence. I thank God for you and all that you are to me.

Michael Canion

TABLE OF CONTENTS

Introduction

It is my hope that to some degree this book will better arm you to do battle with our adversary. We are involved in warfare, but it may not appear to be what it actually is. The bombs that explode, explode in the battleground of our minds.

Satan is in Sales, is really a book about warfare. It reveals how subtle and deceptive our adversary is, as he seeks to slowly and methodically gain a foothold in our lives.

The battle is real, and deceptive in how it's waged. In the Garden of Eden there was warfare; a warfare of words, that targeted mind, to secure her faith.

The salesman came with a presentation aimed at infiltrating the mind of Eve; so that her faith would shift from the truth to a lie.

It is interesting that neither Adam nor Eve had any innate sin principle at work in their lives in the beginning, yet Eve was still deceived. From this we learn just how skilled the salesman is as he seeks to influence our choices. We must put on the whole armor of God that we will be able to stand. I hope this book is a helpful weapon in your arsenal, as we fight the good fight of faith.

Michael Canion

Chapter One

I Know Too Much

One day I was at the Mall, and as I was walking pass one of the restaurants, there was a young lady standing in front of the restaurant with a plate in her hand. On that plate, was a sample of the food they offered. It was not just any sample, it was what they felt was the best they had to offer. As I approached, she came up to me with a smile, and said try one, it is very good. I took a sample and she was right, it was delicious. It is interesting what happened when I ate it though. When I ate the sample, I acquired knowledge that I did not have before. Prior to eating the sample, I knew nothing about how it tasted, I only knew that it looked pleasant to the eye. After I ate it, my eyes came open and I knew something I did not know before. From that moment on, I had to deal with what I knew about how it tasted, and the pleasure it gave to my taste buds. Before I left the Mall, I stopped at the same restaurant to get more of the taste I had come to know. When I had my first taste and preceded to walk through the Mall, I could not ignore or unlearn what I had come to know by experience about how it tasted. The knowledge that I gained was a point of reference that stayed with me the entire time I was there.

When God warns us against certain behavior, it is because there are things that He does not want us to know. Once you come to know something by experience, you may constantly fight against the desire to feed that knowledge with another experience, which is a catalyst to bondage and addition. Initially, in the Garden of Eden, Adam and Even knew good but had no experiential knowledge of evil. The knowledge of evil, and its consequences, was what God did not want them to experience. He knew that they, and we, would forever be fighting against the evil we come to know.

Before I continue with that train of thought, I will go off the beaten path for a moment.
One thing we learn from the sin of Adam is that when their eyes came open, they knew they were naked. They both gain knowledge they didn't have prior to their sin. That begs the question, were they covered with something prior to the knowledge of their nakedness or were they naked all the time but didn't know it, I believe both may be true. While this is just my opinion, I believe they were clothed in the garden, and the garment they wore was innocence. One definition of innocence is, lack of guile and corruption, it carries the idea of purity. A toddler will run around friends and

strangers butt naked and feel no shame because the baby is clothed with innocence. He does not know he is naked, he is innocent of his nakedness.

Genesis 2:25 reads, Adam and his wife were both naked, and they felt no shame.

I think it is significant here that they are naked but shameless. The reason there is no shame is because they are clothed in innocence. The absence of innocence often causes shame. How often have you done things that were wrong, and even though others may not have been aware of it, you felt shame nevertheless. You realized that you did wrong, and in the process, you violated something you knew was right.

Maybe, when Adam and Eve disobeyed God they lost the garment of innocence they had always known, for the first time they knew what it was like to be uncovered. Being uncovered was both foreign, frightening and shameful; shame is the fruit of lost innocence and your sin being exposed.

In John the eight chapter, the man and woman who were caught in adultery knew that what they were doing was wrong: but can you imagine the shame they experienced when their sin was uncovered. There is a different between guilt and shame. Guilt, is more of a legal term. You are guilty when you break a law; however, shame does not necessarily follow guilt. Many times, shame, has to do more with your deeds being exposed and the emotional upheaval you experience because of your guilt. The man and woman caught in adultery were both guilty, but shame came when their guilt was exposed.

Can you imagine what it must have been like for Adam and Eve, their normal changed in an instant. Their world was turned upside down. I can only imagine how pervasive the fear and uncertainty must have been.

I suppose they did the only thing they knew to do, they hid and covered themselves. They were accustomed to a covering, so the fig leaves were their feeble attempt to replace what they had lost. Now, back to my original train of thought.

Before someone experiments with drugs, their eyes are not open to any experiential knowledge of how drugs affect the mind and body. Once they use drugs their eyes come open to this knowledge and they find themselves prisoners of what they know. Before they knew, there was no struggle, but now they struggle because of what they know. Are you struggling with something that you have come to know by experience? There is knowledge that God does not want us to have, because He knows that it can become a lifelong struggle. The experiential knowledge of sin is the cause of much pain.

It's one thing to have intellectual knowledge about something, but quite another to know it by experience. When Adam and Eve came to know sin by experience, it became a problem to them and us as well.

I heard a story about a woman who was trying to lose weight and she often talked about how difficult it was because she loved sweets. She said, "I don't seem to be able to control myself when it comes to sweets". On Valentine's Day she received a gourmet box of candy in the mail. She said to herself, "I'll just throw it away". But instead of throwing it away she decided to eat just one. She convinced herself that once she ate one, her sweet tooth would be satisfied and the rest would be thrown away. She ate one, and another, and another. What was intended to be just one, ended up being the entire box. If she had not experienced the first piece she would have never eaten the thirteenth piece. When she ate the first piece, her eyes were open and she knew by experience how good it tasted. When you know by experience the affect that something or someone has on you, you must fight to leave it or them alone ; you cannot dabble with it, you must be done with it.

The Salesman is a proponent of encouraging you to try something, just one time. Can you imagine the number of people who thought their involvement in a certain thing would be a one-time encounter? But he used that experience as a foundation on which to build. He used the initial knowledge they gained, to set the stage for more. After your eyes come open, your flesh becomes a greater adversary in convincing you that whatever you did is worth doing again, because now you KNOW how it affects you. The flesh uses the knowledge you gained from what you did, to build a formidable case for doing it again.

I arrived at church one day and there was a fellow standing in front of the door. I knew him from the neighborhood because we had witnessed to him often. He had been addicted to drugs for years, and as we talked, he asked a question as though he was thinking aloud. With tears swelling in his eyes, he said, "Rev, why did I try crack the first time"? The Salesman used that young man's initial involvement with drugs and the evil that he came to KNOW by experience as a catalyst toward addiction. He had spent years fighting and losing, against the knowledge of evil. There are some things that we just don't need to know.

After your initial knowledge of evil, your imagination becomes more vivid because it is fueled by an actual experience. Before you knew evil experientially, your imagination may have lacked clarity but after just one time, the knowledge you gained made the imagery much clearer.

A professional football player once talked of how many times he had been offered drugs during his career. He said, "I made up my mind never to touch it because I was afraid I might like it". He rationalized that the best way to deal with drugs was not to. Ignorance is not always a bad thing because the ignorance of evil is a good thing. It is easier to resist things you've never experienced than it is to resist them once you have an experiential point of reference. This is why the salesman wants you to get involved in some area of sin just one time. He knows that you will be fighting the knowledge of your sin, for a long time. I've never heard of a person who has never tried drugs getting addicted to drugs. Drug addiction starts with the eyes being opened to the knowledge of evil.

"The fear of the Lord is the beginning of knowledge; but fools despise wisdom and instruction. My son, hear the instruction of thy father, and forsake not the law of thy mother: For they shall be an ornament of grace unto thy head and chains about thy neck" (Proverbs 1:7-9).

Much pain can be avoided by believing what God says about the consequences, that's wisdom. A child does not have to come to know the pain of being burned if he simply takes the word of the parents that the fire is hot. Adam and Eve had been foretold by God of the consequences of eating the fruit.

Genesis 3:2-3 say,
> "And the woman said to the serpent, 'We may eat of the fruit of the trees of the garden; but of the fruit of the tree which is in the midst of the garden, God hath said "**Ye shall not eat of it, neither shall ye touch it lest ye die**".

If you are struggling with the knowledge of some sin, you cannot undo or suddenly become ignorant of what you know. However, if you confess it and daily ask God for strength, spend quality time with Him in prayer, His word and fasting; He will strengthen you. You can win against the knowledge and power of sin. Just as you came to know sin by experience, you can also come to know by experience that the grace of God is sufficient. Jesus said you shall know the truth and the truth shall set you free. Ignorance of truth is a dangerous thing; but to reject truth is even worse.

Just as the children of Israel gathered manna daily, we must daily get what we need from God in our fight against sin, Satan and the world. I am convinced that in our struggle against sin, prayer, bible study, church attendance and fellowship with other believers are essential. God has and will continue to help us. Many times, out prayer can be summed up in two words, HELP ME.

Isaiah 40:28-31 (NIV)
[28] Do you not know? Have you not heard? The LORD is the everlasting God, the Creator of the ends of the earth. He will not grow tired or weary, and his understanding no one can fathom.

[29] He gives strength to the weary and increases the power of the weak.

[30] Even youths grow tired and weary, and young men stumble and fall;

[31] but those who hope in the LORD will renew their strength. They will soar on wings like eagles; they will run and not grow weary, they will walk and not be faint.

1.When I had my first taste of the food and proceeded to walk through the Mall I could not _____ what I had come to know by experience about how it tasted.

2.Once you come to know something by _____, you may constantly be fighting against the desire to feed that _____ with another experience which is a catalyst to bondage and addition.

3. There is a _____ that God does not want us to have because He knows that it can become a lifelong _____.

4. The Salesman is a _____ of just one time.

5. After your eyes come ____, your flesh becomes a greater _____ in convincing you that whatever you did is worth doing again.

6. After your initial knowledge of evil, the _____ becomes more vivid because it is fueled by an actual _____.

7. Much pain can be avoided by believing what God says about the _____, that's wisdom.

8.Ignorance of _____ is a dangerous thing; but to reject the _____ of truth is even worse.

Chapter Two

Satan is in Sales

When I first got out of the military I didn't know what I wanted to do. While I was deciding the next move, I took a job as a salesman. I learned a great deal about selling, and came to realize that the most important part of becoming a good salesman, took place before you were ever in front of a customer, it took place in the classroom. A good salesman knows his product and the tendencies of the people he is trying to sell it to. Ideally both parties should be satisfied with the outcome of the exchange but that is not always true.

While at this job I came to understand the culture of selling. Selling is all about an exchange, and in order to make the sell, the consumer must feel good about the exchange. In other words, the consumer must believe that what they get is worth what they pay for it.

Many years ago, I had an encounter with a vacuum cleaner salesman who called the house offering to clean the carpet free of charge. The only catch was that my wife and I had to sit through a presentation, that sounded like a good deal. In exchange for my time there was something in it for me, a clean carpet. I had no intention of buying what he was selling, but the moment I decided to sit through the presentation I put myself at risk. The salesman uses the presentation to provide you with information concerning the benefits of what he has to offer. He provides information that targets your senses and stimulates your mind.

When I chose to sit through that presentation and listen to what he had to say, there was the possibility that I would see or hear something that could entice me to decide that what was being sold was something I wanted. He started the presentation by telling us about the company, its reputation and what this vacuum cleaner could do. I tried to act as interested as I could, but in my mind, I was saying "just clean the carpet". Sitting through the presentation was part of the agreement so I had to sit. The presentation consisted of two parts, the verbal presentation and the visual demonstration. When he started the visual demonstration, I saw what it could do and immediately it got my attention. What the presentation did not accomplish by what I heard him say, it did accomplish by what I saw it do. During the visual presentation, my wife and I realized that this was not just another vacuum cleaner. This was the Mercedes of vacuum cleaners. This vacuum cleaner was a carpet shampooer, a leaf blower, car vacuum, wood sander, and paint sprayer among other things. The presentation was so good that when he finished I said, "I've got to have one of these".

Initially, we had no intention of buying the vacuum cleaner, but the presentation was so good that it enticed us to the point where we considered it, and ultimately were convinced that we had to have it. We never would have gotten to the point of consideration had we not consented to entertain the presentation.

However, I consented because I was certain I would not going buy a vacuum cleaner, at least I thought I was certain. As I closed the door behind the salesman and looked at this vacuum cleaner and all of the attachments, I said to myself "why did I buy this thing". Have you ever done something and after the fact said, "why did I do that"? You probably did what you did for the same reason I bought that vacuum cleaner. You put yourself at risk and were overwhelmed by a great presentation. Have you ever been in a situation that may not have been wise, but you felt confident in what you thought your response would be? I gave the salesman the opportunity to influence me when I consented to listen to what he had to say. Companies like this one, spend millions of dollars on their product and gathering information about consumer habits; this information helps them construct a presentation that they feel will be effective.

A well done, insightful presentation is a powerful ally to a salesman trying to make the sell. Once I chose to sit through the presentation I gave the salesman something he otherwise would not have had. I gave him an opportunity. The opportunity did not guarantee that he would succeed, but the lack of an opportunity voids even the possibility of being successful. If the salesman is going to have any chance, you must consent to give him an opportunity. I think the operative word here is consent, because nothing happens without it.

Satan is also a salesman and is constantly making offers, knocking on the door of our minds waiting to see if we will invite him in. He hopes that we will respond by opening the door and entertaining what he has to say to the point of considering the benefits or imagined benefits of what he has to offer. In order to get you to the point of consideration, he knows that you must be willing to listen to **WIFM,** it's not a radio station, it means **W**hat's **in It for M**e? Why do you think I sat through that vacuum cleaner presentation? I didn't sit there because it was something I longed to do. There was something in it for me, a clean carpet. I weighed the perceived benefit against the cost. The benefit was a clean carpet and the cost was my time. The salesman used the offer of cleaning the carpet as an incentive for the purpose of enticement. He offered a free service hoping it would create an appetite for more, and more always costs. The service he offered was not really free because it cost my time initially, and my money later. The presentations purpose is to either create an appetite in you for what is being offered or excite an existing appetite. Satan uses the proposition of personal gain as incentive for you to sit, look, and listen.

Satan was the salesman in the Garden of Eden and he made his presentation to Eve. The presentation was based on the benefit she would receive in exchange for disobeying God. Genesis 3:5 reads" For God doth know that in the day that you eat thereof, then your eyes shall be opened and ye shall be as gods, knowing good and evil"

The salesman in the garden came with an offer of exchange. If this exchange was to occur he had to

convince her that she would benefit. Gen 3:1-5 reads "Now the snake was the most subtle of all the wild animals the LORD God had made. One day the snake said to the woman, "Did God really say that you must not eat fruit from any tree in the garden?" The woman answered the snake, "We may eat fruit from the trees in the garden. But God told us, 'You must not eat fruit from the tree that is in the middle of the garden. You must not even touch it, or you will die.''
 But the snake said to the woman, "You will not die. God knows that if you eat the fruit from that tree, you will learn about good and evil and you will be like God!"

Eve listened to this presentation, bought what he was selling, and the human race has been buying from him ever since. The salesman has not changed his strategy and why should he, if it's not broke don't fix it? He knew that she had to believe in what he offered as a benefit before she would choose what he wanted. She listened to the presentation and when the salesman was finished, Eve was sold.

 Remember, a sale is all about exchange. In the garden, the goal of the salesman was to exchange the object of her faith from what God said to what he was saying. As Eve listened, there was a gradual exchange that happened in her heart and then in her actions. She was convinced concerning the positive impact of this exchange. She believed that disobeying God had benefits beyond those of obeying Him. More importantly, she was deceived into believing that this exchange would come without cost, even though God clearly stated the cost of eating from the fruit of the forbidden tree. We often buy what the salesman is selling without giving any thought to the possible cost. We become the ultimate gamblers when we choose to make a purchase without even knowing how much we will pay.

The salesman in the garden uses the same strategy today. He uses the deceptive offer of gain for the sake of influencing our choices. Deceptive, because the promise never lives up to the hype and there are hidden costs that make the purchase price extremely high. Again, we become gamblers of the highest sort when we make purchases without knowing the extent of the cost, yet it happens every day. The salesman wants you to be so taken by the presentation that you become blind and deaf to anything beyond the momentary gratification of self. Countless lives have been ruined at the expense of an exchange made in the heat of the moment. Marriages have been destroyed, people have been killed, friendship lost, influence lost, all at the expense of an exchange rooted in the momentary gratification of self or the belief that a lie was truth.

The salesman in the garden was concerned with the outcome and there was a process he used then and now because it continually proves to be effective in achieving the outcome he desires. There are three steps in this process, first there is the presentation which we have discussed, secondly, meditation and thirdly, the choice.

MEDITATION

Part two of the process is the meditation. I said earlier that the salesman uses the information to target your senses and stimulate your mind. Your mental participation is necessary in order for him to be successful. This is why the salesman wants you to meditate on whatever you perceive as the benefit of what he has to offer. Meditation involves more than having a casual thought about something. It involves mental focus and preoccupation. The presentation targets your mind and offers you an object of meditation.

When you sin, which basically means to cross a boundary set by God, it all starts in your mind. The sins you commit with your body have already been done in your mind or heart. There are two choices connected to one sin, the choice to sin in my heart or mind and the choice to sin with my body. " Matt 15:19 reads, for **out of the heart** proceed evil thoughts, murders, adulteries, fornications, thefts, false witness, blasphemies". Jesus said "... ye have heard that it was said by them of old time, thou shall not commit adultery. But I say unto you, that whosoever looks on a woman to lust after her has **already committed sin in his heart**". Again, sin is basically disobedience to Gods word, crossing a boundary set by God.

This boundary it is not restricted to the physical act, but also includes the thoughts of the act in the heart. The salesman uses the presentation so that you can see yourself actively involved in what you are being offered. He wants you to entertain what he is offering to the point of mental participation. However, Jesus wants us to know that the moment our thoughts cross a boundary set by God, that is sin. He is teaching us that this desire to cross boundaries must be dealt with at the source; the heart or the mind. The mind must be engaged in thoughts that promote the act. Again, the mind must be engaged in thoughts that promote the act. All our lives we are bombarded with images and desires that seek to influence our thoughts into crossing boundaries set by God. Everyone, concerning something, has been guilty of crossing His boundary at one time or another. When you cross those boundaries, you must acknowledge it, confess it, and repent of it.

Fetal sin

James 1:13-15 says, "Let no man say when his tempted that he is tempted of God; for God cannot be tempted with evil; neither tempts he any man; but every man is tempted when he is drawn away of his own lust, and enticed. Then when lust hath conceived it brings forth sin and sin when it is finished brings forth death ".

James says we are tempted when we are drawn away of our **own lust**. There are different degrees of lust, or desire. The greater the desire the more intense the temptation to cross the boundary. The desire grows as you feed it, because whatever you feed will grow; and whatever you starve will die. It will probably stay dead until you give it resurrection power by feeding it again. You starve your desires by not allowing your meditations to feed them. The less you feed it the weaker it becomes. James says, "when lust hath conceive it brings forth sin". One definition of conceive is to take in one's mind by forming an image of it. When you allow the desire to produce mental imagery it brings sin forth, from the mind to the body, from contemplation, to manifestation.

When a child is conceived in the womb of its mother, it grows until the womb can no longer contain it, then the child is born. Lust is conceived when desire and imagination come together in the womb of the mind and grow until the mind no longer contains it, then sin is born. Sin in the heart is sin unborn. A baby in the womb does not negate the fact of its existence. It is no less a baby because it's in the womb, but we call it a fetus. When the baby is born it leaves the womb and enters the world. Just as a fetus in the womb is no less a baby, sin in the heart is no less sin. Sin in the heart is a phrase of location telling us the place of origin. The heart is where the problem is. Sin is sin whether done in the heart which is spiritual, or with the body which is physical.

But someone may rationalize that if what I have done in my heart is sin, I may as well go ahead and commit the act physically. The knowledge of sin being committed in the heart is for the sake of dealing with it at the source and cannot be used as an excuse to externalize it. The purpose of dealing with sin internally, is so that it won't become external. It's one thing to think about robbing a bank, it's another to actually rob it. While both are wrong, there are be irreversible consequences once you physically commit the act. When you commit the act, you set a law in motion. The law of sowing and reaping. Dealing with sin in the heart can avert some serious consequences.

Sin in the heart must be acknowledged because God sees it. Your thoughts and desires may be hidden from others but they are naked before God and no amount of fig leaves and cover this nakedness. **Genesis 3:7 reads** and the eyes of them both were opened, and they knew that they *were* naked; and they sewed fig leaves together, and made themselves aprons. We cannot hide our thoughts from Him, we must acknowledge confess them. Gods knowledge of the sin in our hearts ought to be a great incentive to confess it, because He already knows about it. There is nothing we can say to God that is a revelation to Him.

In 2 Samuel, the thirteenth chapter we read that Amnon raped his sister Tamar and his brother Absalom hated him for it. Absalom said nothing good or bad about Amnon, but in his heart, he created a video of his brother's death and he replayed it for two years. When the time was right he had Amnon killed. In the heart of Absalom, Amnon was dead two years earlier. Absalom's sin began in his heart and because he did not repent of what was in his heart, he gave birth to what was there. Meditations that tempt us to cross Gods boundaries for us must be aborted so as to stop their birth. Herodious, the unlawful wife of Herod hated John the Baptist with a passion because he spoke out against their sin. She wanted him dead and thought about it often. When Herod made a foolish, ill-advised vow to her daughter, she used that as an occasion to have John beheaded. The problem with Herodious was that her heart was filled with meditations and images of Johns death until at last, she gave birth to her sin. The problem with man is not so much what he does as the heart from which it comes. David's prayer was "create in me a clean heart", his prayer must be ours as well.

Gen 6:5 reads, "And GOD saw that the wickedness of man was great in the earth, and that every imagination of the thoughts of his heart was only evil continually".

One definition of imagination is a mental picture that you form of something that is not present to the senses. The Salesman wants you to use your imagination to create a mental picture of yourself in the act of sin. He wants you to have your own private video.   He says to you look at this, think on it, and agree with me that it's worth having or doing. Satan wants your thoughts to feed your imagination and fuel your desire to the point of no return.

The Bible reads in II Corinthians 10:4-5 "For the weapons of warfare are not carnal, but mighty through God, to the pulling down of strongholds; **casting down imaginations** and every high thing that exalts itself against the knowledge of God, and bringing into captivity every thought to the obedience of Christ." Your flesh is the instrument of your mind; therefore, it is important that the right thing be on your mind. Finally, brethren, whatsoever things are true, whatsoever things are honest, whatsoever things are just, whatsoever things are pure, whatsoever things are lovely, whatsoever things are of good report; if there be any virtue, and if there be any praise, think on these things. Phil 4:8 (KJV)

The Choice
The third part of this process is "the choice". If you meditate on a thing long enough your meditations will influence you to choose to externalize the act.   The ability to choose presents us with the freedom to be selective which carries a great deal of personal responsibility because if you choose wrong it can be costly. I often wondered why God placed the tree of the knowledge of good and evil in the garden in the first place. He placed it there because that was the only way they could be truly free. In order to be free, they had to have an alternative to what God said. The presence of this alternative provided them with the freedom to choose. God did not

want them to eat fruit from the forbidden tree, however, they could use their freedom to do as they pleased, to live as they pleased. Notice that He says to them **Genesis 2:16-17 (NIV)** ¹⁶And the LORD God commanded the man, "You are free to eat from **any tree** in the garden; ¹⁷ but you must not eat from the tree of the knowledge of good and evil, for when you eat of it you will surely die." They were not free by law to eat from the forbidden tree, for the law of God was "thou shalt not eat". However, they were free by volition to choose to break the law.

God encouraged them to use their freedom responsibly and gave the consequences of using it irresponsibly. We live during a time when people are using their volition to live as they please and they are free to do that. We are bombarded with opportunities to use our freedom to choose the right behavior or the wrong behavior; but we must also be willing to accept full responsibility for the choices we make. The fruit of the irresponsible use of freedom tastes sweet until it hits the belly and sour's in our stomach. We are free to use our freedom irresponsibly but we must know that our choices and consequences are linked at the hip like Siamese Twins.

When my son Christian was small he came to me and said, "daddy may I have some more cookies "? I said no, and if you get some I'm going to spank you. I went upstairs. When I came downstairs a little later I went into the den and sat down. He wanted to wrestle so he jumped on my back. While we were wrestling, I noticed that there was some chocolate mixed with

cookie crumbs around his mouth. I said, "
son did you get more cookies ". He looked
as though he was saying, God must have
told him. He reluctantly said, " yes sir ". I
said, "son why did you do what I told you
not to do"? He said, " I don't know ".
Needless to say, I was not satisfied with
that answer.

Tell me I thought I could get away with
it. Tell me yes, I did it but I'll never do it
again, but don't tell me " I don't know ", as
though some strange power overtook you
and guided you against your will into the
cookie jar.

He disobeyed me for no other reason
than he chose to. Getting what he wanted
was more important than doing what I
said. His choice was based on what he
considered the priority at the time. His
priority was self -gratification. To get what
he wanted he chose to disobey me. He
allowed himself to be overcome by the
seductive desire to experience taste of the
chocolate chip cookies. He was free to
choose and he chose wrong. His action was
motivated by thoughts of self- gratification.
It seems that rather than being thankful for
our freedom to choose, we attempt to
relieve ourselves of the responsibility for
our actions by blaming others. In this
respect, we reveal our kinship to Adam.
"And the man said, 'the woman whom
thou gavest me, she gave me of the tree and
I did eat"(Gen 3:12).
Adam seems to blame God and Eve, as though Eve
pried his mouth open and force fed him. Eve may have
influenced him but he chose to eat.

Years ago, a comedian named Flip Wilson was known for the phrase "the devil made me do it". Sometimes we act as though we feel that way as well. It is easier to blame someone than accept responsibility for what we do.

When God asked Adam about his sin, Adam blamed Eve and Eve blamed the serpent. How easy it is to excuse our sins by blaming someone else or our circumstances. When you make wrong choices don't try to cover them by shifting the blame. "He that covers his sins shall not prosper, but whosoever confesses and forsakes it shall have mercy" (Proverb 28:13).

It is human nature to hide our sins or overlook our mistakes. But it is hard to learn from a mistake you don't acknowledge making. To learn from a mistake, we need to admit it, confess it, analyze it, and change our minds in regard to it so that it doesn't happen again. Everybody makes mistakes but not everyone profits from them.

There may be things or people who seek to influence your choices, but the fact is, you do what you do because at that moment you chose to. No one twisted your arm and made you go wherever you went or say whatever you said. If you didn't have the ability to choose, you could rightly say the devil made you do it, but that would be tantamount to demon possession; if this is the case you need an exorcism. If you did not have the freedom to choose, then what you would do remains a mystery to everyone except God. Sometimes the lack of an opportunity is a safe haven from which to criticize the choices of others and declare what you would do.

I once read a story about a professional jewel thief, his street name was Klepto. At one time Klepto was a professional jewel thief, but he professed to be a changed man. He says that for most of his adult life he was one of the best jewel thieves around. He has known other jewel thieves who professed to have stopped, but when presented with the opportunity to do it again they did. But Klepto says that he is indeed a changed man.

Klepto was asked how long had he been a changed man. His reply was "all of fifteen years". Then he was asked how long had he been in prison. He mumbled under his breath and said for fifteen years. Klepto professed his deliverance in the absence of choices to do otherwise. He didn't steal, because he couldn't.

Our freedom offers us an opportunity to demonstrate our willingness to obey God. The world is constantly encouraging us to use our freedom to choose an alternative to the life that God desires for us. Billions of dollars are spent and influence is used to provide a stage for these alternatives. When faced with these alternatives we must believe that God's word is truth and the outcome He promised is sure. If we do not believe the truth of His word, then the alternatives become more appealing. Everyone must ask themselves what they really believe and why they believe it. The answer to these two questions are determining factors in how you choose to live your life. It is not enough to believe something because all over the world people believe things that are not credible; things that have no solid foundation and are not worthy of their faith.

Ephesians 4:27 – "And give no opportunity to the devil".

The salesman may come knocking, but we don't have to answer.

A. The Presentation

1. The purpose of a _____ is to inform you by what you see, hear, taste touch or smell.

2. We never would have gotten to the point of _____, had we not consented to entertain the _____.

3. The presentation gives the salesman something he otherwise would not have, an _____.

4. What does W.I.F.M mean? _____?

5. Satan is in sales and he uses temptation to knock on the door of your _____ while he waits for your response.

6. Satan uses the proposition of personal gain as _____ for you to sit, look, listen.

7. Temptation is not so tempting unless you believe that it _____ you in some way.

B. The Meditation.

1. Mental _____ is necessary for the success of temptation.

2. Most of the time the sins you commit with your body have _____ been done in your mind.

3. Most often when you make the wrong choices, it is because you are _____ about the wrong thing.

4. Your emotional state is directly linked to the object of your _____.

5. One definition of imagination is a mental picture that you form of something that is not present to the _____.

6. Satan wants your thoughts to feed your _____ and fuel your _____ to the point of no return.

C. The Choice

1. The ability to choose presents us with the _____ to be selective.

2. You must _____ to control what you _____ and what you do.

3. We must strive to control our thoughts by practicing _____ thinking.

4. "He that hath no rule over his _____ spirit is like a city broken down and without _____. "(Proverb 25:28)

5. When the _____ of a city are broken down, anyone can enter, because _____ of the access has been lost; the same is true with your _____.

6. When you make _____ choices don't try to cover them by _____ the blame

Chapter Three

The War Room

When I was in the military, there was a room where the general and the top brass would meet, they called it the war room. This was the room where they planned their strategies. It was here that they talked of the enemy's weaknesses and strengths, surprise attacks, and enemy capability. The war room was a place of strategy where the only objective was to win.

The Salesman is a very opportunistic strategist. In Matthew 16:18 Jesus said to Peter, "upon this rock I will build my church and the gates of hell will not prevail against it. In the Old Testament, the gate was a place of authority where civil decisions were rendered. The gates of hell may metaphorically refer to the place of Satan strategy. Strategy is defined as the science and art of military command exercised to meet the enemy under advantageous conditions. When the Salesman shows up that may be a good sign that he thinks has the advantage. "Lest Satan should get an advantage over us; for we are not ignorant of his devices" (2 Cor2:11).

What does the Salesman use to his advantage? Many times, he uses your environment. **He** helps to create or seeks to take advantage of an environment that is conducive to sin. Sometimes you have no control over your environment, at other times you do. As much as possible, avoid environments that can influence you towards crossing boundaries God has set. The enemy can use the environment to appeal to a legitimate desire such as freedom, sexual expression or hunger, but he wants you to satisfy these desires his way.

In Matthew 4:1-11 Jesus was hungry. Hunger is a legitimate desire; but he refused to satisfy His hunger the way the enemy suggested; he chose to wait on God. The stronger the desire the more the environment can intensify the temptation to act independently of God. A person in a grocery store would probably find that his desire to eat would be intensified because of his presence in that environment. We must understand the relationship between desire and environment. Your desires can be intensified by your environment, because the environment offers satisfaction to the desire within us.

There are places you cannot go, people you cannot associate with, and things you cannot watch, hear or touch. When Joseph found himself in a bad environment, he ran. Joseph was a man with the same desires as any other man but he refused to satisfy them by crossing God's boundary. Gen 39:11-12 reads, "And it came to pass about this time, that Joseph went into the house to do his business; and there was none of the men in the house there within. And she caught him by his garment saying lie with me: and he left his garment in her hand, and was fled forth".

Joseph may not have only been running from her, but himself too. If you've got to run to keep your victory, let your parting prayer be, feet don't fail me now.

Another weapon is the arsenal of the enemy is subtleness. He is a master of the subtle. Have you ever stood and watched the hour hand on a clock? You know it's moving, but the motion is so subtle until you cannot really discern any movement at all. But that the hand is a lot closer to the next number than it used to be. Satan uses subtleness to guard against alarming you and shield the progress of his influence.

When I was a child, there was a television program called "Leave it to Beaver". Even though there was a great deal of problems in this country at that time, there seemed to generally be a higher level of morality that was evident in the programming of the day. Whenever there was a bedroom scene, the parents would be fully dressed in pajamas and robes, the robe only came off when they got into their separate beds.

As time passed there were subtle changes in the programs concerning bedroom attire. The robes came off, but that was fine because the pajamas were still on. The pajama shirt came off but that was fine because the under shirt was still on. The under shirt came off but that was still ok because the pajama bottom was on. Now everything is off, and everyone is wondering when and how did we get to this point. It didn't just happen, it had been happening slowly, progressively and subtlety over a period of years. Satan subtly used the influence of the movie makers to make television X-Rated right before our very eyes. He does not seem to be concerned with speed, but with certainty. Anything that happens to fast will cause alarm. He apparently believes the slow way is sure way. Subtlety has the ability to dull our senses to the changes going on around us. Many of the things that are legal today, were illegal years ago. What brought about the change? The changes came as the result of a slow, calculated agenda. The enemy is patient.

People who backslide don't really know when it happened, because the compromises were so subtle. Satan may tempt you to make subtle changes in church attendance, prayer, bible study and your overall environment; he is looking to where these changes can lead. If you dim a light slow enough, you will find yourself in darkness without knowing when it got so dark. If changes happen slow enough you adapt to the level of light you have.

The enemy also uses the power of suggestion. One day when my two children, India and Christian were very small, they were in the den watching television. As they watched television I heard India say as though she was simply thinking out loud, "I sure would like to have some of that angel food cake with whip cream and strawberries". Christian continued to watch television, but then it dawned on him what she had just said and he whispered, "yea".

Before she had mentioned it, he was content to sit and watch Gullah Gullah Island; but that suggestion had changed the object of his attention. It was not long before he was asking anybody who would listen for some angel food cake with strawberries and whip cream. Christian eventually got what he wanted, but guess who also got what she wanted, my daughter India. Her plan had worked to perfection. Suggest what you want, allow your little brother to accept it as his own idea, then he does what you want. The salesman also understands the power of suggestion. He is a master of suggestive manipulation. To manipulate is to control or play upon by skillful means for one's advantage. He does not have the power to coerce or force you to do what he wants but if the environment is right he may influence you to believe that his idea is a good one.

In Genesis 3:1-5, the bible reads, "Now the serpent was more subtle than any beast of the field which the Lord God had made and he said unto the woman, 'Yea, hath God said you shall not eat of every tree of the garden. And the woman said to the serpent, we may eat of the fruit of the trees of the garden? But of the fruit of the tree which is in the midst of the garden, God hath said, Ye shall not eat of it, neither shall ye touch it lest ye die. And the serpent said unto the woman, ye shall not surely die; for God doth know what in the day ye eat thereof then your eyes shall be opened, and ye shall be as gods knowing good from evil".

In these verses, it seems that the enemy may have targeted a pre-existing question to manipulate Eve; that question may have been "why doesn't God want us to eat from this tree?' His suggestion was that God was holding out on them, there was something greater than what they had and God did not want them to have it. Eve meditated on these words and embraced the salesman's idea as her own. She was skillfully manipulated by suggestion. How many times have you been manipulated without even realizing it.

The enemy also uses lies. While serving in the army, there was a fellow in my company, let's call him Bill, who took a great deal of pride in his ability to lie; as though that is something to be proud of. He had become such a profound liar that even though you knew he was the consummate liar, he was so convincing that sometimes you would think, maybe he is telling the truth this time. I often wondered how in the world someone could lie like that; then I read about *his father*. Jesus said to the Pharisees in John 8:44,"Ye are of your father the devil, and the lust of your father you will do. He was a murderer from the beginning an abode not in the truth, because there is no truth in him. When he speaks a lie, he speaks of his own for he is a liar, and the Father of it". The primary weapon in the arsenal of the Salesman, is the lie. Just look at how many times he has lied to you. He probably said you are not going to make it, you can't live holy, nobody cares about you, nobody will ever marry you because you're so overweight or, if God loved you He would have done something by now. Remember, he is a liar. He has an aversion for the truth.

Truth has to do with agreement between what is said and the outcome. When a lie is told there is no agreement between the two; this is why whenever you believe a lie you will always be disappointed. The salesman is a tremendous promoter, and he specializes in hype. He offers you things with the promise of satisfaction and fulfillment, then after the fact he laughs and says surprise. He is a perpetual liar always enticing us to believe that we can find true fulfillment in what he has to offer. What He offers as the path to fulfillment simply pacifies the flesh and creates a cycle of dependence and disappointment.

Lies and disappointment go hand in hand. Only Christ can fill that void in your life and satisfy the longing of your soul. Can you imagine Eve's disappointment when she bit into that fruit? Eve was disappointed because she believed a lie and was given a false hope. If you are to avoid disappointment, then you must believe that everything God has said is truth; therefore, the outcome he has promised is certain.

When you embrace a lie without realizing it, you can begin to live the lie. Living a lie is like making a wrong turn while driving; each mile takes you further and further from your intended destination. You will end up somewhere, but not where you thought. . When you base your life on a lie, the only thing that you will experience is pain, disappointment and a sense of futility. If you believe that you are useless, you will live as if you are useless. If you believe that you are ugly and unloved, you live like it. If you believe a lie to be truth, the result can only be disappointment. If you have been living a lie for any length of time, it may be difficult for you to accept the truth about who you are in Christ. But why is it so difficult to accept the truth about who we are?

The difficulty in accepting truth, is the result of the momentum and strength the lie has gained from being enforced by repetition; repetition in thought and action. Every day you live a lie, the lie gains momentum and as the momentum increases, the lie becomes a lifestyle. God's word concerning you is truth, but truth must be received before it can bring about change. You must accept the truth about the new creature you have become in Christ. The liberating power of truth can overcome the momentum created from years of living a lie, if truth is received.

It says in 2 Corinthians 5:17, "If any man be in Christ, He is a new creature: old things are passed away, behold, all things are become new".

Even though you are a new creature in Christ, there may still be remnants of the influence developed while living the lie; whatever lie you may have been living.

In Mark 4:35-39 we read that there was a great storm raging while Jesus was in the hinder part of the ship asleep. After Jesus was awaken from His sleep, the Bible reads in verse 39, "And He arose, and rebuked the wind, and said unto the sea Peace, be still. And the wind ceased, and there was a great calm".

When Jesus spoke to the wind, He dealt with the source of the problem; but the waves of the sea were still contrary because of the influence the wind had on the water. Even though the source of the problem had been alleviated, its influence was still present in the form of waves. The same thing Jesus used to alleviate the source of the problem, He used on the influence that was left. He used His word. The living word has the innate power to deal with the source of the problem and any influence that is left.

The moment He spoke to the sea there was instant calm. Why is it that His word many times doesn't have such an immediate impact in our lives? I believe it is because we allow our feelings about ourselves or our situation to resist what He has said. When He spoke to the sea it had no will with which to resist His word. You and I have a will, and when things seem contrary or overly difficult to overcome, we choose to resist rather than receive. Seed thrown on the sidewalk will never bear fruit because the concrete cannot receive it. Our unbelief is the concrete that stops the word from bearing fruit. We resist the seed of God's word when we do not accept the truthfulness of what He has said, and His word cannot bear fruit where it is not received.

> "For unto us was the gospel preached as well as unto them: but the word preached did not profit them, not being mixed with faith in them that heard" (Hebrews 4:2).

For some reason, we tend to think that because of how we feel about our situation or how things appear, His word is ineffective. Feelings can never be trusted when it comes to determining truth. Sometimes you may not feel saved but your salvation is not dependent on your feelings. Likewise, your victory in whatever area is not dependent on whether or not you feel victorious.

Feelings are unstable and ever changing, but God's word is forever settled. You are victorious because God says you are, believe it. If you have problems believing it, pray, and ask Him to help you overcome unbelief. Whatever lie you have been living, the truth will make you free. You may not feel free but that is fine, because your freedom is not a feeling it is a fact. It is also extremely beneficial that you don't surround yourself with people who validate the lie you have been living. Every lie seeks a support system. We all need someone in our lives who will tell us compassionate truth; our victory is in receiving truth.

As you accept His word as truth, it not only deals with the source of the problem it deals with influences that may yet remain. There is a song that says, "I am who God says I am". The salesman has lied to you and influenced you to believe that you are who he says you are, and when your faith empowered the lie you began to live it. A lie has no power other than the power we give in with our faith. Without your faith, the lie stands idly by, powerless to affect you. Without your faith, the lie sits on the bench, itching to come into the game, but he needs your faith in order to play.

Lastly, He uses division. We are many members but one body by virtue of our union with Christ. What affects one part of the body affects the entire body. Whenever one part feels neglected by the other part, Satan may use this neglect as a source of division.

Act 6:1 says "And in those days when the number of disciples was multiplied, there arose a murmuring of the Grecians against the Hebrews, because their widows were being neglected in the daily ministration".

This neglect, if not dealt with, could have caused serious divisions in the body of Christ. But the wisdom of God through the Apostles prevailed.
Acts 6:3-5 says "Wherefore brethren look ye out amongst you seven men of honest report, full of the Holy Ghost and wisdom, whom we may appoint over this business. And the saying pleased the multitude: and they chose Stephen, a man full of faith and the Holy Ghost; and Philip, and Prochorus and Nicanor and Timon and Parmenas, and Nicolas a proselyte of Antioch. Spirit filled men were chosen to deal with this issue of neglect.

We have allowed Satan to skillfully use our differences in gifts, economics, education and race to divide us. When in fact, it is the presence of these differences that allow the body of Christ to function without handicap. The feet are different in appearance from the hands but the difference between the two is what makes them so needful. Just as the body without feet is handicapped, so is the body of Christ handicapped when we do not appreciate the preciousness of our differences.
I have never seen a person who stubs his toe, and the rest of the body is oblivious to the pain; that is, unless the person has been drugged. Sometimes we live as though we are under the influence of pre-Christian ideology and prejudices, which are harmful to the health of the body. It is past time to rid ourselves of this drug, that has proven to be toxic, causing us to be weak and sporadic. A drug that has made the body numb to the pain of the parts. We must acknowledge our

oneness, appreciate our differences and minister to the pain of the part in need. We are one and we need each other.

As I look over the landscape of our nation, I see so much division. Why have we not become one, or at least achieved a greater degree of unity? Why are we yet so segregated? I believe that most of it may have to with the pre-conversion influences that yet dominate our thinking and decision making. We have not, nor do we seem to be concerned, with sanctifying ourselves of those thoughts and ideals.

I believe the racial divide is perhaps one of the most prolific weapons in the arsenal of the enemy. The power of a truly unified church, would have such a far-reaching impact for Christ, that we would literally be in awe of its effect. What would happen if the world saw the diversity of the church on display, moving as one man, in love; the love that Jesus talked about. We tend to talk about many different things, but love does not seem to be a priority. This is interesting, because without love, we would yet be in our sins. Love was the motivation for our salvation. For God, so loved the world that He gave His only begotten Son, that whosoever believes in Him, should not perish but have everlasting life. John 3:16

I often wonder, what would happen if we truly loved one another as Jesus said we should, not just tolerate one another, but love one another. We seem to want to be a Christian, until we are challenged to change, challenged to love each other, but Jesus was always challenging the status quo.

1. _____ is defined as the science and art of military command exercised to meet the enemy under advantageous conditions.

2. The _____ the desire the more the environment _____ the temptation to act independent of God.

3. We must understand the relationship between _____ and _____.

4. Satan is a master of _____ manipulation.

5. When a lie is told there is no _____ between what is said and the outcome; this is why whenever you believe a lie you will always be _____.

6. What Satan offers as the path to fulfilment simply _____ the flesh and creates a cycle of dependence and disappointment.

7. _____ a lie is like making a wrong turn while driving; each mile takes you further and further away from your intended destination.

Chapter Four

I've Got to Have It

Every day we are inundated with advertisements and commercials declaring that we must have what is being advertised. Your life is not complete unless you have this; you will never be the same once you try that; everyone else has one so you need one too. These commercials are designed to appeal to or create a sense of inadequacy. There is nothing like a car salesman trying to convince you of how good you look behind the wheel of that new car. He says, when this car came off the assembly line it had your name on it. So, you sit inside and whiff that new car smell and almost agree that 'I've got to have it'. You are tempted when something appeals to your sense of inadequacy. And because you feel inadequate there is a desire to be adequate. The intensity of this desire may overshadow morality or ability and allow the end, the possession of the coveted object or person, to justify the means for how you acquire it.

In the third chapter of Genesis, Eve may have wondered why God placed a prohibition on the fruit of the tree of the knowledge of good and evil. But it was only after a Satanic suggestion that she felt inadequate. Sometimes you feel very adequate in Christ until Satan, your flesh or someone else suggest that you're not. Eve failed to realize that in God she had no lack, she was whole. Sometimes, we too are guilty of looking for a relationship, material possessions or status in your group to give us a sense of adequacy. Since these things cannot give us what we really need, we are ever reaching and never attaining. We must realize that the Christ in us is enough. It is very important that we realize this, for then we know that whatever we have, or accomplish, can add nothing to us for in Christ we have no lack. Satan tempts us to doubt the sufficiency of God through Christ in our lives. He tempts you to reach beyond the boundaries of God's word to secure what you have in His word; sufficiency. YOU ARE NOT INADEQUATE.

SUFFICIENT IN CHRIST
Temptation is basically a test of your faith in the sufficiency of God through Christ. The Greek word for sufficiency is *arkeo* which mean to be enough. Because all of our needs are met in Christ, He is enough. Sometimes we say God I'll do this or I'll do that when I get enough. God says do it I am enough.

Paul prayed that the Lord would remove his thorn in the flesh, but the Lord responded by saying

> "My grace is sufficient [enough] for thee; for my strength is made perfect in weakness" (1 Corinthians 12:9-10). Having received this revelation Paul says, "most gladly therefore will I rather glory in mu infirmities, that the power of Christ may rest on me".

While there may be some debate concerning what the thorn was, there are some things that are not debatable. We know that he had it, we know he didn't want it, and we know the Lord wouldn't remove it. I think that when we go overboard emphasizing the thorn, we are distracted from the primary message of the passage. The message is, whatever you are contending with in your life, God can use it as an occasion to demonstrate the sufficiency of His grace by enabling you to do what needs to be done in spite of it. God will prove to be enough in the midst of and in spite of your situation. We would all love to have ideal situations, I would. But realistically, most situations in our lives are not ideal. Anything less than ideal is met with the prayer "take-it-away-from-me". But very seldom does it leave and if it should, it doesn't leave fast enough for us. The Lord uses these less than ideal circumstances to demonstrate His ability through us, causing us to know by experience that His grace is sufficient.

Some years ago, my sister was brutally murdered. It was strange that a few months earlier she said, "you know Mike when I die I want you to preach my funeral". She said jokingly, "I want you to put me away really good". We laughed and I said, "you got it". Little did I know that the time would come much sooner than either of unexpected.

Because of the circumstances surrounding her death and the manner in which she died, I experienced a wide range of emotions; grief, anger, and depression. On the morning of the funeral it seemed as though all of these emotions converged on me at once. I was in no shape to preach a funeral. I said, "Lord help me", and He did.

I found that I could through Him. He enabled me to do what needed to be done in spite of myself and everything that contributed to the situation. He proved to be sufficient. Sometimes you may feel that you can't go any further, you just can't take anymore. But you find that,

"He giveth power to the faint and to them that have no might He increases strength (Isaiah 40:29)".

God used my weakness as an opportunity to demonstrate His sufficiency through me. The emotions were still present, but He enabled me to do what I had to do in spite of them. It's as though the Holy Spirit shifted into override and enabled me to do what I had to do, in spite of my feelings. We serve an in spite of kind if God. How many times has he enabled you to go on in spite of yourself and everybody else. Sometimes we may feel as though we cannot go on in the absence of things we don't have, and the presence of things we don't want. But God can use the absence of one and the presence of the other to reveal the sufficiency of His grace through us by manifesting his power.

Paul said,
"But we have this treasure in earthen vessels that the excellency of the power may be of God and not of us" (2 Corinthians 4:7).

The vessel can take no credit, because in the absence of the power the vessel is useless.

Because of His power, things that would otherwise overwhelm and destroy us does not. Paul testifies to the sufficiency of Gods enabling grace by saying.
"We are troubled on every side, yet NOT distressed, we are perplexed yet NOT in despair; Persecuted, but NOT forsaken; cast down, but NOT destroyed", (2 Corinthians 4:8-9).

The key word in these two verses is "not". Because the grace of God through Christ is sufficient, the things that we faced did NOT have the ultimate effect that Satan intended.
How many times can you look over your like and say to the salesman, you thought you had me but, NOT.
"Not that we are sufficient of ourselves to think anything of ourselves; but our sufficiency is of God" (2 Corinthians 3:5).
As unpleasant as they sometimes are, the presence of trails and temptation give us the opportunity to know by experience that Christ is sufficient.
"And God is able to make all grace abound toward you; that ye' always having all sufficiency in all things, may abound to every good work" (2 Corinthians 9:8).

1. The _____ of this desire may overshadow _____ or ability and allow the end, the possession of the coveted object or person, to justify the means for its achievement.

2. Eve failed to realize that in God she had no _____, she was _____.

3. And many times there may be things done in the name of the _____ that are really done in order to give us a sense of _____.

4. Satan tempts us to doubt the _____ of God through Christ in our lives.

5. Sometimes we may feel as though we cannot go on in the _____ of things we don't have, and the _____ of things we don't want.

6. As _____ as they sometimes are, the presence of trials and temptation give us the _____ to know by experience that Christ is sufficient.

Chapter Five

It Costs Too Much

When my wife goes to the grocery store, shopping is not just something to be done, it is something to experience. I prefer to sit in the car, because I know she is going to be a while. She is very cost conscious and takes as much time as necessary to get the most for the money. I sit in the car and wait, and wait. Finally, she comes out with a lot more than I ever would.

Whenever I go to the grocery store my plan is simply get in and get out as quickly as possible, I just don't like shopping. This plan is primarily concerned with time and not so much with the cost. Sometimes I am not very cost conscious and end up paying too much. When I come home and my wife looks at what I have and how much I paid; she says, "you paid too much for this". You know that you have paid too much when what you get is not worth what you paid.

There can be a tremendous cost when you give in to the salesman. When you are tempted, he wants your desire to reach such a fever pitch until cost is a non-issue and you presume upon the mercy and forgiveness of God. We must understand that while He is a forgiving God, forgiveness does not negate consequences. Sin carries consequences. Sin can cost you the loss of your health, loss of influence, and the loss of your life. When faced with temptation you must look beyond the perceived benefit, to the cost. By considering the cost it may help you regain the proper perspective in regard to temptation, and influence you to do the right thing.

David's sin with Bathsheba and murder of Uriah came at a great cost. For a moment let us look at David's diary. Well, one evening, I had just gotten up from taking a nap when I decided to go on my roof and enjoy the remainder of the evening. Joab my general had gone with the army to do battle with Ammon. I should have been there but I decided to stay home this time; after all I knew Joab was a very competent and seasoned man of war.

As I got to the top of the roof I was thinking about where God had brought me from. I was a blessed man. I was the King. I walked toward the edge of the roof and from my vantage point I could see a woman bathing. My first thought was to turn away but I didn't, she was one of the most beautiful women that I had ever seen. I felt somewhat ashamed as I invaded the privacy of this woman. But I said to myself, I am the king, as though being the king justified what I was doing. Power and influence can be an intoxicating cocktail and while under the influence you tend to believe that the rules that apply to everyone else don't apply to you. I was so captivated by her beauty that I convinced myself I had to have her. So, I slept with her. She was the wife of another man but I slept with as though she was my own. I knew what I did was wrong but the knowledge of it being wrong did not stop me from doing it. My imagination fed my lust to the degree that the desire to do wrong overruled my desire to do right. Not one time did I think about consequences or the possible cost I would have to pay.

Later, she informed me that she was pregnant and I didn't know what I was going to do. I tried my best to cover it up but everything failed. I could not risk being exposed so I devised a plan. I would have her husband killed, marry her, and no one would ever know, so I thought. I had not counted on the all-seeing eyes of God.

God told me through the prophet Nathan that He was aware of what I had done. When I was with Bathsheba there was pleasure but ultimately the pain far outweighed the pleasure. Did it cost too much? The son that I had by Bathsheba died. My son Amnon raped his sister Tamar. Absalom, another of my sons killed his brother Amnon because he raped Tamar. My son Absalom, the son of my flesh tried to kill me. Was it worth it? What do you think? The price I paid for giving into temptation was staggering. As I looked at my family disintegrating, I knew it was because of me; my sin affected more than me. The consequences of sin do not stop at your door but visits the many doors of those connected to you. The pleasure I received from my sin was not worth the cost. When you give in to temptation you make a purchase without knowing how much you will pay. If I had thought beyond what I desired to how much it could possibly cost, things would have been much different. I was so blind by what I wanted that I never thought in terms of cost. Count the cost of your actions and you will save yourself much grief.

God is so gracious and longsuffering that many times He may not discipline us immediately for the sins we commit. He loves us so much that in His mercy He gives us time to repent. Instead of being thankful for His patience with us and repenting, we take His grace for granted and we are emboldened to do it again; but all unrepentant sin seems to draw interest.

Roman 2:4-5 reads
>'Our despises thou the riches of his goodness, and forbearance and longsuffering, not knowing that the goodness of God leadeth thee to repentance? But after thy hardness and impenitent heart treasurest up unto thyself wrath against the day or wrath and revelation of the righteous judgment of God" (Romans 2:4-5).

As we looked at David's diary now let us look at Samson's diary. My name is Samson. From the day I was born, I was set aside as a Nazarite. According to the Nazarite vow, I was to touch no dean thing, drink nor eat anything from the vine or cut my hair. I was young, handsome, and when the Spirit of the Lord would come upon me I was strong enough to do anything I wanted because I was anointed.

The anointing of God attracts people to you, some good, and some bad They know there is something special about you because of how you do what you do. They don't understand that it isn't you at all but God working through you. I was so accustomed to my strength that I began to take it for granted. The women were crazy about me and I was crazy about them. Whenever the guys saw me they had to talk to me because most of them wanted to be like me. There were some who didn't care for me but they wouldn't say it to me. One day as I was walking, a lion came against me, I broke his neck. Sometime after that, I came by the same way and there was the carcass of this same lion, but it was full of bees and honey. I knew that I was not to touch any dead thing, but the honey looked too good to pass up so I got some. The Spirit of the Lord was still with me though, because I later killed thirty men of Ashkelon. The more I think about it, since God did not withdraw Himself from me, rather than thanking Him for being so merciful, I became confident that I could sin again.

I remember the time I was at a wedding feast. I knew that anything from the vines was off limits to me but again I yielded to temptation. The guys were saying things like, is this the mighty Samson who conquers men but runs from wine, so I drank the wine. Through all of my disobedience the Spirit of God was still upon me. I guess I thought that delayed judgment meant no judgment, so I continued to give in to the temptations.

Then I met this woman named Delilah. I said to myself "this is the one". She stood head and shoulders above all the other women. I had no idea that she was working with the Philistines to find the secret of my strength. I did notice that she was preoccupied with finding out what made me so strong but I didn't think much of it. She kept asking and asking, until I became weary of her and finally, I told her. When I told her, my sin was complete.

While I slept during the night she cut my hair. When she finished she stood by the door, let the Philistines in and yelled, Samson the Philistines be upon thee. I jumped up as I had done before ready to defend myself. But this time there was something different. I looked the same. I jumped to my feet as I had done so many times before. Unlike before, there was something different this time; this time the Spirit of the Lord had left me and I was an ordinary man. I had never known fear but now I was afraid. If someone were to ask me to define fear I would say that fear is knowing that God's mercy has ended and His Spirit has departed. I was captured by the philistines and my eyes were put out. Because I continually gave in to temptation, I was left a broken man. Did it cost too much? Absolutely. I keep telling myself it didn't have to happen this way. When you are tempted to give in to the salesman think about me. It cost too much.

1. Can you think of a time when you paid too much? _____

2. What do you think you learned from it?

   _____

3. Did it change how you make decisions, if so, in what
   way?_____

4. Do you think David regretted what he did even before he was exposed?
   Explain_____

5. How do you think you would have handled it?

   _____

6. Do you think Sampson took his anointing for granted? If so why

   _____
   _____

7. Have you ever taken what God has done in your life for granted?
   When_____

8. Did you ask for forgiveness?

   _____

Chapter Six

Time to Amputate

The patient lay on the bed. During the course of the examination the doctors reached a unanimous conclusion. The leg must be amputated. These words pierced the patient like an arrow. He panicked, how could this be he thought. He began to scream and fight the doctors until he had to be sedated.

When he came out of sedation the doctors explained that if they did not amputate, the infection would spread throughout his body and he would die. After thinking about the consequences of the leg remaining attached to his body, he consented to the amputation. Amputation involves the severing of a relationship. The relationship between the infected leg and the rest of the body had to be severed. After the leg was severed the patient had to deal with the pain of the amputation. The pain was most severe when the leg was initially amputated, but with each passing day it got better and better until it was healed. The patient found out that he could live without the leg; as a matter of fact, that was the only way he could live.

If you continually yield to temptation you could find yourself in a relationship that is just as infectious. You must consider the cost of keeping the relationship it will cost your anointing, it will cost you pain, anguish, guilt, and it could cost your life. It's time to amputate.

Jesus said in Matthew 5:30,
"And if they right had offended thee, cut it off, and cast it from thee: for it is profitable for thee that one of thy members should perish and not that thy whole body be cast into hell".

Jesus is saying that there is a time when certain relationships must be severed. There are some things and some people that you must cut away.
Paul says it like this in Hebrews 12:1, "Wherefore seeing we also are compassed about by so great a cloud of witnesses, let us lay aside every weight and the sin that so easily besets us".
The patient in our story panicked because he could not imagine himself living without his leg. After all they had been together a long time and the relationship with his legs was not always bad; it once was a healthy relationship.

You know when a relationship must be severed. At one time the relationship was healthy, but now sin has set in and spread, and the only way to survive is to amputate.

The patient had to consent to the amputation. The doctors were there ready and willing to help but they could not do it against the will of the patient. He had to sign a consent form. It was not enough that it needed to be done, he had to want it.

Ask yourself a question. Do I really want this relationship severed? God is standing by waiting to help you; knife in hand. Will you consent? He will not work against your will. The question is "wilt thou be made whole"? It is written in Isaiah 1:19 that

"If you are willing and obedient, you shall eat the good of the land".

Once you consent to sever the relationship, you must perform the surgery quickly. The longer you wait, the worse it gets. Procrastination is an ally of the infection. (2 Corinthians 6:2)

The man consented to the amputation. The leg was amputated. It was painful. The necessity of amputation does not negate the pain involved, but it's better to be in temporary pain among the living than in the grave among the dead; because infections can kill. But the longer you abstain from involvement, the intensity of the desire becomes less and less. Abstinence robs desire of intensity because the desire of the flesh is not being fed by ongoing experiences. Each experience feeds the desire, and makes more vivid one's imagination.

When the leg was severed from the patient there was no chance that it would be reattached. When you sever an infectious relationship, you must guard against attempts at reattachment because the possibility does exist. The fact of amputation does not negate the possibility of future temptations to reattach. But the longer you abstain from involvement it lessens the intensity of the desire to reattach, making the temptation easier to resist.

The amputation must be complete. There is no such thing as a partial amputation. But you say we will just be friends. You cannot be friends with an infection because it has the potential to kill. If you do not completely sever the relationship you are setting yourself up for reattachment to something that could eventually be devastating.

Sometimes in spite of your knowledge concerning what is right, it may not be easy to do. The knowledge of what's right does not mandate that it will be easy to perform. Right things are not always easy things. Look at Jesus. He knew what was right to do, but it was not easy to do.

Luke 22:42-43

> "Father, if thou be willing, remove this cup from me: nevertheless, not my will, but thine be done. And there appeared an angel unto Him from heaven, strengthening Him".

It may not be easy but God will strengthen you. The amputee was eventually healed and got along quite well without the leg. You too will come to know by experience that you didn't need that leg anyway. It's time to amputate.

1. Amputation involves the _____ of a relationship.

2. Are there unhealthy relationships that you need to sever? _____

3. If you answered yes, what are you going to do about it. _____

4. The _____ found out that he **could live** without the leg.

5. You must _____ the cost of keeping the relationship, it may cost your, it will cost you pain, anguish, guilt, and it could cost your life.

6. Seeing we also are _____ about by so great a cloud of witnesses, let us **lay aside every** _____ **and the** ___ that so easily besets us".

7._____ is an ally of the infection.

8.What is it in your life that you need to cut away?

Chapter Seven

Wait

Metropolitan Atlanta has seen a boom in the population. People from all over are moving to Atlanta, and you see it every day in the amount of traffic we have here. There was a time when rush hour was at certain times during the day, now, rush hour seems as though it is every hour of every day. Traffic is so bad that you plan your day around the traffic, it can be frustrating, you just have to be patient.

I was in traffic one day, moving at a snail's pace, it was

hot, and if that wasn't bad enough, my air conditioning was out. The car felt like an oven, I was sweating and traffic wasn't moving. As I crept along in that hot car, I decided to take action. There was a street to the left just ahead and I decided to make the left, go the back way through the neighborhood, and come out further down the road. When I got to the street, I made the left, a right, another left, and came back to the intersection of the street I had turned off of initially. To my surprise, all of my driving savvy had put me even further behind that I would have been if I had just been patient, and waited. To make it worse nobody wanted to let me in, they just looked straight ahead, as though I wasn't even there. These people were tired frustrated and were not about to let me in. I tried to look in their faces hoping that somebody would be merciful, but this was not a merciful crowd.

Waiting, being still when you feel like you've got to do something, can be extremely difficult; but as in my case, activity does not mean progress. Sometimes, one of the greatest temptations is to move when we should be still. If I had just sat in the traffic and moved with the flow, however slow, I would have been further along. It is easy to teach and preach sermons about waiting, but the hard part is to actually wait. Waiting is especially hard for people who by nature are just action oriented, they must be moving.

I remember, one time a couple came to me and wanted to get married. They had not known each other very long so I suggested that they wait, at least six months or so. I just did not feel good about it. I thought that our time together went well and believed they were receptive to what I said. The following Sunday they came to church stood up during praise and testimony service, some of you may remember when we had testimony service, and said they were married. They were smiling and holding hands. I guess the counseling didn't go as well as I thought. I can't tell you how often single people have clapped, stood and said amen about waiting within the context of a relationship. But many times, they agree with you because they are not in a relationship at the time. Once they get in a relationship all of that waiting talk goes right out the window.

About two months later, I got a call at two in the morning, it was the same brother who married the young lady. He was at a phone booth, that lets you know how long ago that was, I don't know if they even have phone booths anymore. He said his wife had jumped on him and ran him out of the house. He wanted me to call her and see if see would let him come back home. They were married about six months and got divorced.

There is a positive side of waiting that seems to be minimized or neglected altogether. The salesman is always close by, whispering in your ear, saying, you don't have to wait, do it now, this might be your last time.

In 1 Samuel 10:8 ,Samuel says to Saul,
Go down ahead of me to Gilgal. I will surely come down to you to sacrifice burnt offerings and fellowship offerings, but you must wait seven days until I come to you and tell you what you are to do." In this verse, the prophet tells Saul where to go, Gilgal, what to do, wait, and how long to wait, till I come. I don't think you can get any more exact than that. God wanted Saul to know what to do, but waiting was a prelude to knowing. He had to wait on God through the prophet. But what does it really mean to wait on God? To wait on God doesn't mean that you do nothing, it means to do only what you have been told. Waiting on God does not mean complete inactivity, it means activity within the context of your instructions. You wait on God when you do no more, or less, that you have been told.

Saul had been given, precise, exact instructions. He knew what to do; but the knowledge of what to do does not make it easy to do. It takes a great deal of strength and faith to wait. I pray that God give us all the grace to not only wait, but wait well. Saul went to where he was supposed to go, and stayed there seven days, but he did not wait for Samuel to arrive. He was so close, but close is not good enough. Disobedience to a part of the instructions is disobedience to the whole of the instructions.

The Philistines had gathered to wage war, his men were deserting, and Samuel had not yet arrived. The operative words here are, not yet. Saul panicked, and took it upon himself to offer sacrifices, which was only to be done by the priest, Samuel. As soon as he offered the sacrifices, Samuel came. Most times, panic induced decisions are not the right ones. The answer may not have come yet but that does not mean it's not coming. Impatience forfeited Saul's rule over the kingdom. It seems that God often uses waiting to stretch, test and enlarge our faith. It is often in the wait that we are tempted to abandon faith.

Many times, Gods answers are strategic in nature therefore waiting is necessary. The length of time you wait is not indicative of a failed promise, it is indicative of a promise whose time has not come, so again, waiting is misunderstood.

Abraham and Sarah misunderstood the wait and proceeded to take matters in their own hands, and gave birth to Ishmael. The problems in the middle east today, is the result in large part to their refusal to wait. How many times have you given birth to an Ishmael because you misunderstood the wait and took matters in your own hands.

Mary and Martha misunderstood the wait as Jesus purposely waited until Lazarus sickness ended in death and his body was in a tomb, four days. It is so easy to misunderstand why we must wait since we don't have God's perspective or understand His purpose. The operative word here is purpose. There is divine purpose connected to the wait.

Since we do not have His perspective or understand His purpose, we must trust Him, trust is the place of peace. When we trust in God's love for us, and trust the wisdom of His ways, there is peace. The cure for anxiety while waiting is trust.

Your waiting is not punishment. Your waiting is purposeful. Don't allow the enemy to incite panic or anxiety because of the longevity of your wait. The wait is working in your favor, for your good and His purpose. The wait is WORKING in your favor. Wait on Him and He will strengthen your heart, wait, I say on the Lord.

1. Do you find it difficult to wait, explain?

_____

2. Do you sometimes feel that waiting is passive, explain? _____

_____

3. How has impatience worked against you?

_____

4. Do you believe that when you don't know what to do, you should just wait? Or, are you more prone to take action even when it is not clear what action to take, explain? _____

5. What is your favorite scripture that deals with waiting? _____

6. Why do you think it is your favorite?_____

_____

Chapter Eight

Who's Got The Influence

In the military, the purpose of a reconnaissance mission is to simply observe the enemy and gather as much information as possible. It is not a mission whereby you seek to engage the enemy, it's all about gathering information that will be useful in developing your strategy.

I often wondered why the Salesman approached Eve and not Adam. Could it be that through observation he learned that the best way to get to Adam was to get to the one who had influence with him? Influence, by definition, is the capacity to have an effect on the character, development, **or behavior** of someone or something. In order to affect how someone behaves, you must have influence.

What I am about to say, I cannot be emphatic about, because the bible is not specific on this matter. This is purely conjecture, but it does seem plausible, because the bible clearly states in 1ˢ Timothy 2:14, "And Adam was not deceived, but the woman being deceived was in transgression". Since Adam disobeyed without being deceived, his behaviour had to have been influenced by something or someone, and Eve was the only someone there.

Maybe, Satan observed that Adam's weakness was Eve. She had influence with the one he was after, so perhaps, his strategy was to use her influence against him. It would not be an unreasonable assumption, because the enemy understands the power of influence.

As a child, your parents may have warned you against hanging around certain kids, they did so because they realized that you could get in trouble hanging with the wrong people because of their influence.

I was watching the news one day and a story came on about a young man who was an honor student, a good son and a hard worker. He became friends with a fellow who was a gang member and he eventually joined the gang. While trying to commit a robbery, he shot and killed a man. Two lives ended, one in death and the other in prison. What happened? He allowed the wrong person to have influence in his life. There are things you may not ordinarily do, however, if the wrong person has influence in your life you may find yourself doing those very things.

I have seen people in church fall under the influence of someone, and the person uses that influence to affect a behavioral change in the person. Influence is all about having the power to move people in the direction you want them to go. I believe that God is going to hold us all accountable for how we use our influence. There is such a tremendous responsibility that comes with having influence.

Scripture often warns us to avoid harmful influences. Regardless of our age or spiritual strength, over time, unwise influences will negatively affect our walk with the Lord. Satan is determined to pull us into sin and wreck our lives, and he often uses wrong influences to accomplish his goal. Who has the influence in your life? The answer to the question is important, because many times, your decisions are the result of that influence.

When Satan tried to get Job to curse God, he used Job's wife to say what he wanted, "curse God and die" was her declaration to Job. It was fortunate for Job, that while she may have had influence with him, it was not enough to move him to do that.

King Solomon, in spite all his wisdom, married women that God warned him against; and they turned his heart after other gods. How did this happen? It happened because they had influence on him, and used it to get what they wanted. When they used their influence on Solomon, the decisions he made regarding the nation and worship was a result of their influence. You don't have to be the head of a nation to change it, just have influence with the one who is.

1 Kings 11:1-3 reads, "King Solomon, however, loved

many foreign women besides Pharaoh's daughter—
Moabites, Ammonites, Edomite's, Sidonians and
Hittites. ²They were from nations about which
the LORD had told the Israelites, "You must not
intermarry with them, because they will surely turn
your hearts after their gods." Nevertheless, Solomon
held fast to them in love.³He had seven hundred wives
of royal birth and three hundred concubines, and his
wives led him astray".

It seems that a large part of Satanic strategy is to target
people and institutions that have influence. If you want
to influence the masses, you must infiltrate people and
institutions that have influences over the masses.
Television, printed media, radio, governments, all of
them affect masses of people. He seeks to use that
influence to promote his agenda.

We also, as leaders in the Lords church must be mindful
of how we use our influence because we all have
influence, to different degrees, but we have it
nevertheless. All of us have targets on our back,
because the enemy knows that the fall of a Christian
leader has a ripple effect. If the enemy can influence
Christian leaders to move away from the gospel of
Jesus, to a new gospel, they can use their influence to
cause others to move as well. Your influence can either
draw people to God or drive them away from Him.
May God help us all to be strong, wise and vigilant.
Leaders are just as frail as the people they lead, this
mandates that leaders spend quality time with God.

I am happy to see Christian movies coming to the big
screen because for too long, the enemy has been and
still is active in Hollywood, promoting his system.
Hollywood has seemingly has desensitized us to
violence to such a degree that we are saddened by the
violence that occurs in real life, but not shocked

anymore, because we have been fed such a steady diet of violent images. The games children play are violent. Television and many of the movies are violent. It's no wonder that we are seeing so much violence acted out. Mass killings, gang violence, road rage and just the overall disregard for human life is so prevalent that we are at a loss for words.

If we believe in God, and we do, we must also believe in the existence of Satan, The Adversary of God and His people. Children cannot go to school and learn without the fear of being killed. Some politicians are presenting measures that will allow teachers to be armed and others want students armed. There is so much fear, and fear is fertile soil for Satan. How have we come to this? It has happened slowly, gradually the enemy has been moving his agenda forward; using those under his influence to relax moral constraints.

At some point, you must come to grips with the fact that there is an unseen hand at work, using his influence in the lives of people to create an atmosphere of fear, violence and deception. I watched one the video games that a young person was playing and the level of blood and gore was unsettling even for me. I thought to myself, this unsettles me, but not the child. It seems that repeated doses of so much blood is desensitizing our youth to it.

Anything or anyone who influences you to act in a way that is not consistent with scripture, is bad company. Nothing good happens from bad company. Not long ago I read this illustration on hanging with the wrong crowd. "One day a farmer grabbed his shot gun to shoot at a flock of pesky crows. Unfortunately, he didn't see his sociable parrot that had joined the crows. After firing a few shots, he walked over to the fallen birds and was surprised to find his parrot badly ruffled with a broken wing. When the farmer's children saw the injured bird, they asked, "Dad, what happened?" The farmer simply replied, "Bad company." Source Unknown

1. Have you ever allowed the wrong people to have influence in your life, if so why?

_____

_____

2. Do you ever take the influence you have for granted, if so why?

_____

3. How would it affect how you use influence if you knew you would be held accountable?

_____

4. Do you believe that negative acquaintances influence you? _____

5. Do you think you are a good influence or bad?_____

6. Do you watch or listen to things that could be a bad influence on you?_____

7. Do you think you use your influence to glorify God, explain?_____

Chapter Nine

I Quit

Hell rejoices at the sound of a saint who says two words, five letters, I quit. I Quit! Two words, five letters, but they carry so much weight. I Quit. Two words, only five letters, but because of them, destinies have been aborted and outcomes have been changed. These are the words that the salesman whispers and encourages you to say when life is less than pleasant. He says, the way has been too hard, the price too steep; it has exacted too great a toll, these two words can stop it all, just say, I quit. Greater men than you have said it. There is no shame in these two words if they can stop the pain, he says.

Quitting, have you ever been tempted to quit? The fact that there is even the temptation to quit, speaks to the fact that you started something: you are moving toward something. Quitting renders all of the progress you've made, useless. People who never start anything are never tempted to quit. The temptation to quit comes to those who are doing something. If you are tempted to quit, you must be moving toward something; and you encountered obstacles along the way; obstacles that seem insurmountable. Truth is, obstacles are unavoidable, and I believe necessary. Necessary in that they test your determination to reach your goal or maintain your faith. Anything untested, cannot be trusted.

When you become weary and faint in your minds, the enemy will at times present quitting as a reasonable, viable option. When you quit, all effort ceases, you are not willing to go any further, you have reached the end of your rope and refuse to try and hold on any longer. I quit., I've gone as far as I'm willing to go at this job. I have gone as far as I'm willing to go in this relationship. I quit. My pursuit of the goal has taken such a toll, I quit.

Scripture teaches us that we have need of endurance that after we have done the will of God, we might obtain the promise. Endurance to bear up under the pressure. Endurance to finish what you start. God wants you to be a finisher. The salesman wants you to be a quitter. You need endurance to be a finisher, to outlast the obstacles and carry you through the temptation to quit.
Thoughts of quitting may come when the trials are severe, and God seems distant.

Well, what am I to do when I feel like quitting? The biblical response, is to rejoice. James 1:2-4 reminds us, "My brethren, count it all joy when ye fall into divers temptations; Knowing *this*, that the trying of your faith worketh patience. But let patience have *her* perfect work, that ye may be perfect and entire, wanting nothing". The word patience here is endurance. We can rejoice because various trials can produce endurance in us.

I remember the first time I read this, I didn't understand the rational. How can I count in all joy when I am in an environment where all hell is breaking loose? I had not been saved long and I did not understand how that was even possible, or practical. I understood it even less, when I read about the environment in which the people lived when this command was given.

Over a century before this time the Roman general Pompeii made divisions in Judean territory and made many Jewish peasants landless. The outrageous taxes of Herod the Great drove many small farmers out of business. Fathers were not able to adequately provide for their families. Each day, men would leave home in search of work and return home to anxious wives, only to give them the bad news of an unproductive day. When they could find work, they were paid bare minimum and many times their wages were simply withheld. This is what James addresses in James 5:4-6, "The wages you failed to pay the workmen who mowed your fields are crying out against you. The cries of the harvesters have reached the ears of the Lord Almighty. You have lived on earth in luxury and self-indulgence. You have fattened yourselves in the day of slaughter. You have condemned and murdered innocent men, who were not opposing you".

In Rome grain shortages often lead to rioting. The Jews were being oppressed not only by the Romans, but by the own countrymen as well. They had no voice and they were tired. They were tired of being treated like second class citizens, tired of living in the ghetto, and tired of feeling that God had forsaken them. They had given up so much to follow Jesus and they were tired enough to quit. Some, thought that the price of following Christ was far too high; they didn't realize that the cost of quitting was even higher. If you leave Jesus where can you go.

In John 6, many of those who followed Jesus were challenged by His words because they heard spiritual words with carnal ears; therefore, many of His disciples quit following Him. With so many having quit, He looked at the twelve, and said, will you quit also? It was then that Peter asked one of the most insightful, far reaching questions, and proceeded to give an equally powerful explanation. To the question of, will you quit also, Peter says, quit, where shall we go if we quit following You. Peter proceeded to give an equally powerful explanation as to why quitting was not an option. He says, "You have the words of eternal life. We believe and know that you are the Holy One of God".

That's it in a nutshell, if you leave Jesus where will you go. Just for a moment think about those who did quit. They followed up to a point, but when they were challenged by what they did not understand, they quit. How often does the temptation to quit come, when our understanding of God's ways is past finding out? For a moment, think about the cost of their quitting. Their loss cannot really be quantified because it was so great, great beyond words.

Here we see the relationship between quitting and loss. When you quit you forfeit the future goal. They had the privilege of walking with God, did not value it, so they quit. They quit on God. What a sad commentary for those "who no longer followed Him".

Now, back to the environment into which the book of James was written. In this environment of despair, a group called the Zealots gained popularity, because they wanted to revolt against Rome, and their call for revolution was gaining momentum. In was in this environment of despair that James says, "count it all joy." It would be easy to say, I don't think so; but to understand why he could give such a command you must understand Christian joy. I mentioned earlier that we can rejoice because of the endurance being developed in us; but we can also rejoice because of our eternal perspective.

Christian joy is also the result of an attitude of rejoicing because we live with an eternal perspective.
Our life on earth is but a tiny speck on the timeline of eternity. There is infinitely more disparity between a human lifespan and eternity, than there is between a drop of water in all the oceans of the world combined. Our lives and choices must be governed by the eternal. We tend to place a higher value, and make a higher investment into those things that are passing as opposed to those things that are permanent.

Our perspective is the reason we can rejoice in the midst of trouble rather than quit because of it. Our joy is based on our eternal relationship with God through Jesus, the operative word being eternal. The joy of this relationship is not diminished by circumstances, no matter how negative. I am not saying that we don't hurt. I am not saying that we don't cry. I am not saying that we should live in denial about the presence of pain. What I am saying is the word of God and the Holy Spirit help us realize that one is temporary and the other is eternal. When we view our struggles, strains and pains through the lens of eternity, we regain focus, and we don't quit.

Everything we see, no matter how great or seemingly invincible, has an expiration date, it is temporary. Look at the great empires of the past, at their height, they seemed as though they would exist forever. Yet, all that is left are ruins, the pitiful remains of what once was.

During times of great trials, when the enemy says quit, we must force yourself not to focus on the temporary nature of the pain, but rather the eternal nature of the promise, our eternal relationship to God through Jesus. There is so much in this world that seeks to distract us from focusing on eternity, but when we do, we can count it all joy.

Our pain will have an end, but our eternity with God will not. Eternity is too big to put our intellectual arms around it so, by faith we must believe.
Jesus died once, and rose from the dead never to die again, therefore, He lives forever. By faith in what God has done through Jesus, His death becomes our death, and His life becomes our life.

Pain and death have an expiration date. John wrote in Revelation 21:4, (NIV) "He will wipe every tear from their eyes. There will be no more death or mourning or crying or pain, for the old order of things has passed away." Can you imagine, no tears, no death, no crying or pain? That is extremely difficult to imagine, because that is all we have ever known. We have a history of pain, death, and crying. We know them all too well.

Sometimes, it is difficult beyond comprehension to believe that one day, pain will be eliminated; because our history with pain has been so long. Our joy is in the promise of eternity. Just the thought of eternity makes you say as John said in Revelation 22:20, "even so come Lord Jesus". We are to rejoice in anticipation of His coming. Christian joy is not rejoicing in the car we drive, house we live in, or clothes we wear; all of these things are temporal and shallow. We are thankful for everything that God gives us, but we rejoice because we live in hope of being with Him throughout eternity. The car can be wreaked, the house can burn, but He has promised that where He is, there will we be also.

Because our joy is based on an eternal relationship, we don't quit. Our glace must be on this world, and our gaze on God. We are gazing at things we cannot see, but our faith in His word is the assurance that they are there, so we don't quit. We rejoice in hope of our future with God. 2 Corinthians 4:18 reads "While we look not at the things that are seen, but the things that are not seen, for the things that are seen are temporal but the things that are not seen are eternal. When the salesman whispers, quit, we must consider the promise of eternity. "For I consider that the sufferings of this world are not worthy to be compared with the glory that shall be revealed in us". Romans 8:15

Our joy transcends the trouble when we consider the promise of eternity. This is why in Acts 16:25, Paul and Silas could be joyous in prison. This is also why you and I can say as the poet said "though all others flee, I still have thee, and because of this I do rejoice.

1. What are some reasons you have been tempted to quit?

   _____

   _____

2. Are you the type person who has a history of quitting?

   _____

3. Have you ever asked God to help you overcome your propensity to quit?

   _____

4. Do you have the understanding of Christian joy? How will that understanding affect you moving forward?

   _____

   _____

5. Have you ever though in terms of eternity?

   _____

6. Do you make decisions based on an eternal perspective?

   _____

A WORD FROM BISHOP CANION

Even though this is not a book on prayer or evangelism, I include the invitation for people to be saved. I donated hundreds of copies of this book to a prison ministry, and a few months later, I received a request for more. I was told that the prisoners were blessed so much by the book, that they passed it on, from one to another. I wanted to make sure that they would also understand their need to be save, and explain in an abbreviated way, why they needed to be saved. You never know in whose hands a book may fall; this is why there is an invitation to receive Jesus as Savior.

Also, I include the "Thirty Day Prayer Devotional" in every book. Prayer is the thread that is woven throughout the Christian life. I believe that as we become more committed to prayer we will become stronger and wiser in every area of our lives. Prayer is one of the primary weapons in the arsenal of the Christian. Therefore, anything that helps to jumpstart or strengthen our prayer life, is a great help in spiritual warfare.

I believe that no matter what the topic of discussion, inviting the unsaved to receive Jesus, and encouraging the saved to pray, always has a place.

The Invitation

One day, I was walking in a grape vineyard. The grapes were ripe and plump so I reached and plucked some from their branches. I wiped them off with a handkerchief and ate some. The rest, I took home and placed them in a fruit bowl, in the kitchen.

Once I got back home, and in the grind of life, I forgot about the grapes. At some point, much later I went to the kitchen and noticed that the grapes were discolored and shriveled. What happened that brought about the change in appearance?

Let me explain what happened, when I was in the vineyard and plucked the grape from their branches, something happened to the grapes, it was not immediately obvious, but something happened nevertheless.

What happened, was that the grapes died. You see, the moment I plucked the grapes from the vine, the grapes were separated from the life of the vine and they died. Death, is basically the separation of one thing for another. Physical death, occurs when the immaterial part of you separates from the material body, relational death occurs when two people who were once in a relationship or married, separate or get a divorce; so, death is separation. The grapes died the moment they were separated from the life of the vine.

When a link in the chain was broken, they died. Previously, the roots received life from the earth, the vine received life from the roots, the branches received life from the vine and the grapes received life from the branches. The chain was broken when the grapes were separated from the vine.

They didn't look dead, didn't feel dead, but in spite of appearances, they were dead. It took some time before the symptoms of death were evident, but after a while, they became discolored, shriveled, and began to show the evidence of decay.

In the Garden of Eden death came, and we all have been living under a death sentence. Disobedience separated man from the life of God. In our youth, we don't look like we are dying; we are strong and energetic.

Whether it comes in our youth, or, whether we are blessed with long life, it comes. As time passes, we too become discolored and shriveled. Our steps become shortened, our sight dims, our skin wrinkles and our pains come more frequent in occurrence, and varied in location.

We are all dying. Regardless of your race, your economic status, power or prestige, you are dying. The rich die, the poor die, black, white, brown, yellow, we all die. The resurrection of Jesus was His response to death. So many people are asking, is Jesus relevant today? As long as there is sin and death Jesus is relevant.

Today, I want to extend the invitation for you to receive what God has done through Jesus, that you might be saved, saved from the finality of death by experiencing the resurrection life of God through Jesus. As Christians, we die, we just don't stay dead. We live with the promise of the coming resurrection.

One day, the hand of death will reach for us, and lay hold to us, but it won't be able to maintain its grip. Just as it could not hold Jesus, it won't be able to hold us, it has to let go. The resurrection of Jesus assures us, that death has to let go. For the Christian, there is life beyond the grave. Today, confess Jesus to be your Savior, believe from you heart that He rose from the dead, and live as though He is your Lord. He came that you might have life and that more abundantly.

If you received Jesus as your Savior, it is vitally important that you connect to a local congregation of believers. Connecting to a local church is crucial to your growth as a Christian. May God bless, keep and strengthen you.

30 Day Prayer Devotional

Devotion carries the idea of giving time to God for the sake of developing intimacy. The goal of this devotional is to assist in jump starting your prayer life. Hopefully, it will be a catalyst toward intimacy with God. Over the next thirty days, it is my hope that your fellowship with God will go to the next level.

How to use this devotional.

1. Be sure to read one devotional daily. Whether you feel like it or not, read. Do not compromise your devotional time.

2. Read the devotional and then be silent.

3. Begin to think on what you have read, think deeply and allow the Holy Spirit to speak to you.

4. Write down what you feel the Holy Spirit is saying to you in regard to what you have read. The journaling aspect is extremely important.

5. Revisit those thoughts and feelings throughout the day.

Monday

"The closer you get to God, the closer you realize you need to come; you are therefore constantly coming toward Him. Each step you take is one less step you have to make. Lord, grant us the grace to keep coming."
 Michael Canion

When it comes to prayer, you realize that no matter how close you get to God, you don't fully apprehend Him, but you are continually blessed in your pursuit of intimacy. Through prayer, God blesses you in your pursuit of Him. The blessings of the pursuit, provides the passion to continue on your journey into intimacy.

How does this speak to you?

_____

_____

_____

Father, grant me the grace to keep pursuing intimacy with You, help me persevere. Enable me in my pursuit of You, by the power of the Holy Spirit.

Tuesday

"Whether the desire for prayer is on you or not, get to your closet at the set time. Shut yourself in with God, wait upon Him, seek His face, realize Him, pray."
– R. F. Horton

Don't allow your feelings to dictate your pursuit of God. Sometimes you feel like praying, and at other times you don't. Your feelings are ever changing, but your need of God does not. Prayer is not based on a feeling but on need, and you need God at all times. The goal is to always pray, whether you feel like it or not.

How does this speak to you?

_____

_____

_____

Father, help me walk in victory over my feelings. Help me understand that faith overcomes feelings. Father, help me to always pray.

"The time you spend alone with God is not wasted, it changes you and it changes your surroundings. To live the life that counts, and have power for service, one must make time, take time, to pray."
– M.E. Andross

Sometimes it may appear that prayer is an exercise in futility, a waste of time. Prayer is not a waste of your time, it is an investment of your time that will yield tremendous dividends. It may seem like a waste of time, because the results most times are not immediate. Don't allow the wait to convince you that prayer is a waste. The farmer who plants his crop does not consider it a waste because he has to wait.

How does this speak to you?

_____

_____

_____

Father I thank you because I know the time I spend with you makes a difference. It makes a difference in me, and my circumstances, whether I can see a difference or not, something is happening. Father help me believe that there are things happening that I cannot see.

"Make time to pray. The great freight and passenger trains are never too busy to stop for fuel. No matter how congested the yards may be, no matter how crowded the schedules are, no matter how many things demand the attention of the trainmen, those trains always stop for fuel."
– M.E. Andross

Many times, life seems extraordinarily busy. Everyone is pulling on you and, you are frustrated, and feel as though you have nothing else to give. Could it be that you have not scheduled a daily time to refuel in the presence of God? You are running on empty, because you have allowed the demands on your life, to crowd God out. Let today be the day you refuel. Time spent with God is often a panacea for everything that ails us.

How does this speak to you?

_____

_____

_____

Father help me to slow down and realize the priority that prayer must have in my life. Help me realize the need I have to pull away from the crowd that I may spend time with You, be refreshed by You and become more like You.

Friday

"You must begin to believe that God, in the mystery of prayer, has entrusted you with a force that can move the Heavenly world, and can bring its power down to earth."
– Andrew Murray

You do what you do because you believe what you believe. Your belief system is what motivates you to act or not. Today, examine what you really believe about prayer and why you believe it. If you don't pray consistently, there is a reason. Many times, the reason is because there is something you wanted that you didn't get. But when it comes to answered prayer, you must trust in the wisdom of God's answer to your prayer. Trust is the place of peace.

How does this speak to you?

_____

_____

_____

Father help me overcome my unbelief. Help me to know and believe in the power of prayer. There are times I struggle with such deep and intense bouts of unbelief, and I seem powerless to overcome on my own, help me overcome my unbelief.

Saturday

God owes you nothing. Whatever He gives comes out of His grace and not a debt He owes you. He freely gives what you cannot earn and do not deserve. On your best day, you can't earn it and on your worse day you can't forfeit it. Grace is the gift of the ages
-Michael Canion

We live in a culture where many people act as though God is indebted to them. God is not indebted to you, you are indebted to Him. He paid a debt He did not owe, you owed a debt you could not pay. You are indebted to the One who paid in His blood for your salvation. Serve Him as an expression of love and appreciation for what He has done. When you pray, remember His grace, and be thankful.

How does this speak to you?

_____

_____

_____

Father, thank you for being so gracious to me. There have been times when I took Your grace for granted and acted as though You owed me something, forgive me.

Sunday

I have been driven many times to my knees by the overwhelming conviction that I had nowhere else to go.
- Abraham Lincoln

It is true that many times life has a way of driving us to God. There are times we come to Him only as we are driven. Jairus was driven to Jesus because of a sick and dying daughter, had he not been driven, he may not have come. Your drive should come from the deep need within you, and the not calamity surrounding you.

How does this speak to you?

_____

_____

_____

Father, today I come to You because I realize how deeply and completely I need You. My need of You is not increased because of calamity or decreased because of calm. I need you equally as much at all times.

Monday

"Satan does not care that you read about prayer if only he can keep you from praying."
Paul E. Billheimer

One of the primary goals of the enemy is to keep you from praying; he does not care if you talk about it, or study it, just don't do it. Today, purpose in your heart to recommit to prayer. Jesus said, "men ought always to pray and not faint".

How does this speak to you?

_____

_____

_____

Father help me to discern the different ways the enemy is trying to keep me from prayer. Help me be sensitive to his strategy that I might be victorious.

What should I do when I don't have a mind to pray? Sometimes the man does not have the mind, but pray until the mind comes. Don't think that you must feel like it to do it. Prayer is a spiritual law that must be obeyed, therefore, it is not contingent on how you feel.

How does this speak to you?

_____

_____

_____

Father help me realize that my need to pray far outweighs any feeling I have that war against my need to seek You. Father, help me win in spite of how I feel.

"The little estimate you put on prayer, is evident from the little time you give to it."
– E.M. Bounds.

You would probably pray more often, if prayer had a higher priority in your life. Your actions are rooted in your priorities. This month, choose to let prayer become a higher priority

How does this speak to you?

_____

_____

_____

Father, forgive me for how little time I have spent with You and help me come to grips with my own unwillingness to pray.

"The one concern of the devil is to keep you from praying. He fears nothing from prayerless studies, prayerless work and prayerless faith. He laughs at our toil, mocks at our wisdom, but he trembles when we pray."
– Samuel Chadwick

The enemy is actively striving to keep you off your knees. He whispers that prayer is a waste of time. He says, God does not really love you. All of this begs the question, why is he so consumed with trying to keep you from praying? He knows that when you pray, he suffers. Make him suffer

How does this speak to you?

_____

_____

_____

Father help me be consistent in prayer. Help me overcome every satanic opposition to my desire to seek You. Help me be mindful of why the enemy wants me to refrain from prayer. Help me to know, I am powerful on my knees.

Friday

"I would rather teach you to pray than to preach."
– Charles Spurgeon

It is interesting to me that the disciples never asked Jesus to teach them to preach, but teach them to pray. They recognized the inseparable link between His power and his prayer life. Today, let their prayer become yours.

How does this speak to you?

_____

_____

_____

Father teach me how to pray, how to commune with You, and how to become more intimate with You. I may outgrow many things but I will never outgrow my need to be taught by You. Lord teach me to pray.

Spurgeon's "boiler room". Five young college students were spending a Sunday in London, so they went to hear the famed C.H. Spurgeon preach. While waiting for the doors to open, the students were greeted by a man who asked, "Gentlemen, let me show you around. Would you like to see the heating plant of this church?" They were not particularly interested, for it was a hot day in July. But they didn't want to offend the stranger, so they consented. The young men were taken down a stairway, a door was quietly opened and their guide whispered, "This is our heating plant." Surprised, the students saw 700 people bowed in prayer, seeking a blessing on the service that was soon to begin in the auditorium above. Softly closing the door, the gentleman then introduced himself, it was none other than Charles Spurgeon.

How does this speak to you?

_____

_____

_____

Father, I pray that today you will help me go to my boiler room and create some heat for today.

Sunday

After you have prayed, you must trust in the wisdom of God's answer. Michael Canion.

When it comes to prayer, trust is the place of peace because Gods answers are wiser than your prayers. Paul prayed that the thorn would be taken away from him; but the answer he received was the message of grace to deal with the thorn.

How does this speak to you?

_____

_____

_____

Father, help me trust in the wisdom of Your answers to my prayers. Help me believe that what You allow or disallow, give or withhold is for my good and serves Your purpose. Sometimes, I struggle with trust, help me overcome my struggle.

God prepares a man for the public in the privacy of the closet. "Out of a very intimate acquaintance with D. L. Moody, I wish to testify that he was a far greater prayer than he was preacher. Time and time again, he was confronted by obstacles that seemed insurmountable, but he always knew the way to overcome all difficulties. He knew the way to bring to pass anything that needed to be brought to pass. He knew and believed in the deepest depths of his soul that nothing was too hard for the Lord, and that prayer could do anything that God could do."
– R. A. Torrey (Emphasis added)

How does this speak to you?

_____

_____

_____

_____

_____

_____

Father, help me to see that just as the root of a tree is unseen but it is the foundation on which the root stands so is prayer to me. Help me develop a strong root system through prayer.

"You will never truly seek God until you realize how destitute you are without Him."
– Michael Canion

The depth of your need of God must become real to you before you will ever truly seek Him. If you don't seek Him regularly it is because you have not come to grips with the depth of your need. Your need of God is so deep that there are no words in any language that can adequately describe it. You must seek Him because you need Him.

How does this speak to you?

_____

_____

_____

Father help me to realize that my need of You is even deeper than I know. Help me realize the depth of my spiritual poverty; and, that this realization will drive me to You every day, starting today.

On persevering prayer: "Look at a stone cutter hammering away at a rock a hundred times without so much as a crack showing in it. Yet at the 101st blow it splits in two. I know it was not the one blow that did it, but all that had gone before.

Prayer is often a cooperative effort. What I mean is that each prayer works in conjunction with the previous ones; this is why you must always pray. Each prayer adds timber to the building. Today, refuse to be discouraged and continue to hammer, to build, to pray.

How does this speak to you?

_____

_____

_____

Father, sometimes I get so weary. It seems that my prayers are making no difference, yet in my heart, I somehow know they are.
Help me stay the course. Help me to be as the stone cutter and realize that this stone will break.

"Time is the price of intimacy."
– Michael Canion

The time you give to God is consistent with the value you place on the pursuit of intimacy. You do what you do, when you do it, and how often you do it, based on the place it holds in your value system. If you value intimacy with God, you will manifest it by spending quality time with Him.

How does this speak to you?

_____

_____

_____

Father forgive me for not giving You the time that You deserve and I need. Sometimes I allow life to consume my time to such a degree that I am left with nothing to give to You. I give the world the precious morsels of the best that I have and give You crumbs. Forgive me for allowing life to crowd You out. Father, I do believe that in the pursuit of intimacy with You, there is no substitute for unhurried time with You."

Friday

"Hurry is the enemy of intimacy."
– Michael Canion

We live in such a hurried world, and many times you have brought the hurry of the world into prayer. Your thoughts are continually racing to the things that you need to do. You can scarcely fall to my knees in prayer before you are ready to rise. Hurry, so subtle, so deceptive, is your enemy when it comes to developing intimacy with God.

How does this speak to you?

_____

_____

_____

Father, today I vow to slow down. I have been a captive in the prison of hurry. Today I will be a captive no longer. I will slow down. When I am tempted to return to the prison that once held me, gently remind me that hurry is my enemy.

Saturday

When it comes to waiting on God it is not a matter of how long you wait but how well you wait."
– Michael Canion

Prayer and waiting are mostly inseparable. He who prays well must learn to wait well. It is often in the wait that you are tempted to believe that prayer is a waste of time. You want what you want, when you want it, much like a small child. You must learn to trust in the wisdom of the wait. There is a reason you are waiting. You must trust, that while it may be uncomfortable at times, there is a reason for the wait. In the final analysis, the wait is working in your favor. When you approach a red light, you stop and wait; to move forward when you are to wait can be disastrous.

How does this speak to you?

_____

_____

_____

Father help me to wait well. Help me to know that the wait is working for my good; and help me resist the temptation to move forward when You have said wait.

Sunday

Whatever comes, trust God with the outcome.
-Michael Canion

Trust is the place of peace. Today, trust God with the outcome of the situation you are facing; after all it is the outcome that really counts. Life can be like a puzzle with a thousand different pieces, trust God to bring each piece together and make them fit in the right place. Trust God With The Outcome!!!!

How does this speak to you?

_____

_____

_____

_____

_____

_____

Father, many times I don't see how things will work out for me; but I know that You are in control. Help me trust You with the outcome. Help me trust that You will cause all things to work together for my good.

Monday

So often when it comes to prayer, we have a sprinters mindset when it ought to be that of a marathon runner. Very seldom do answers come quickly, and when answers don't come when we think they should, we are tempted to quit praying. Pace yourself and stay the course, so that you can finish well. It honors God when we finish well. Keep Praying!!

How does this speak to you?

_____

_____

_____

Father, help me to run this race with patience. Help me to develop the proper mindset concerning prayer. Help me understand that waiting is worship.

Tuesday

No soldier waits until the battle starts before he begins to prepare for it; if he waits its already too late. If you wait until the crisis comes before you pray, you are too late. Prayer prepares you for the coming battle.

How does this speak to you?

_____
_____
_____
_____

Father, help me develop a prayer life during peace-time so that when wartime comes I will be ready.

When you don't feel like going to work you go anyway, because there is value, there is benefit attached to having a job. When you don't feel like praying, pray anyway, because there is value, there is benefit attached to prayer. Pray anyway
– Michael Canion

_____

_____

_____

Father, help me to always realize the value and privilege of prayer. Help me overcome every argument that my flesh, the world and Satan has that seeks to devalue the power and privilege of prayer.

Thursday

When you go to work and complete a task you can see the results of the time you spent. There are times you pray and see nothing, but the time is not wasted. Prayer is an investment of time, not a waste of time and it pays tremendous dividends. The dividends are paid over time, so after the investment has been made you must wait on the Lord.

How does this speak to you?

_____

_____

_____

Father, today I realize that the time I spend with You is the greatest investment of time I can make. Today, I vow to invest more.

Friday

Answered prayer is strategic and time sensitive, because the answer will impact more than you. Zechariah, the father of John the Baptist prayed many years for a son. It was not until he and Elizabeth were very old, that their prayer was answered. The answer to their prayer was strategic, because John had to be born when he could be the forerunner to the ministry of Jesus.

How does this speak to you?

_____

_____

_____

Father, help me trust the timing of Your answers. Help me rest in the assurance that the wait is in Your will.

When you stand praying, forgive. To forgive can be the most difficult of things to do. But why is it so hard to forgive? Forgiveness is most difficult for those who forget how often they have been forgiven by God. Often, you would rather focus on the sin against you, as opposed to the lifetime of sins that God has forgiven you of. When you stand praying, forgive as you think of how much and often God through Jesus has forgiven you.

How does this speak to you?

_____

_____

_____

Father, forgiveness has not been easy for me; but with Your help I can do all things. Help me have a forgiving spirit.

Sunday

Sometimes, it is so obvious that You are with me. However, there are times when I stretch my neck and squint my eyes, trying to get a glimpse of You, and don't see You anywhere; yet I know You are present with me. The proof of Your presence is that I survive. I may not feel You, or see You, but I know You are closer than near to me; You are here, with me, right now.

How does this speak to you?

_____

_____

_____

Father, You promised never to leave me and I know that You are faithful to Your word. Today I will rest in the assurance of Your promise.

Monday

When it comes to prayer, it is better to have a heart without words, than words without heart. Words without heart are words that miss the mark. The heart is the hand that reaches out to God. Reach out to God with your heart. He wants your heart.

How does this speak to you?

_____

_____

_____

Father help me be mindful that You want my heart. My words are empty if they have no heart in them.
Help me to never allow my prayers to be void of heart.

Tuesday

There are times when you realize that you need help navigating the rough waters, dark valleys, and high mountains of life, but there are other times when you feel that you can handle it. One of the greatest realizations you can have is to realize that you constantly, consistently need God. When you feel as though you can handle life without seeking God, you are deceived. You need Him today, all day, every day, for a lifetime.

How does this speak to you?

_____

_____

_____

Father, help me always be aware of how deeply and completely I need you. Help me grow closer to You that You may impact my life more and more.

Prayer is perhaps your most powerful expression of humility. By praying you are submitting yourself under God, you are expressing your subjection to and dependence on Him. You can only be humble when you recognize how deeply dependent you are on God. A humble person is a submitted person.

How does this speak to you?

_____

_____

_____

Father, help me to have a humble and be quick to recognize pride. Help me have the heart of Jesus, who was humble beyond description.

Thursday

The power of prayer lies in its ability to change things, change you, and change people, that left to themselves would not change. We must believe in the power of prayer in order to keep praying when there is nothing we see that gives us hope that change is coming.

How does this speak to you?

_____

_____

_____

_____

_____

_____

Father, help me believe that prayer does change things whether I see any evidence of change or not. Help me to know that my evidence, my title deed to change, is my faith.

About the author

Bishop Michael Canion, Sr. Pastor of the Assembly of Truth Family Worship Center, is the husband of Dr. Tanda Joy Canion, father of two wonderful children, India Nichole and Christian Michael Canion, grandfather of three Lyric Nichole, Nikai Answorth, and Peyton Michael. Bishop Canion is seasoned in the word of God and brings a wealth of experience to the ministry. He received a BA in Biblical Education from Beulah Heights University. Bishop Canion has authored several books, Satan Is In Sales, When Prayer Seems to Fail, Help my Child Read and Things Every Christian Should Know.

Bishop Canion's ministry at the Assembly of Truth Family Worship Center began in the living room of his mother's home. His ministry branches out as follows:

- Senior Pastor of The Assembly of Truth Family Worship Center
- Founding Bishop of the United Fellowship of Churches.
- Ministerial Trainer
- Guest on TBN
- Telecast on AIB
- Contact Bishop Canion
- 404-228-6969

www.bishopcanion.org - - www.assemblyoftruth.com

98942522R00078

Made in the USA
Columbia, SC
07 July 2018